HEALING
THE MIND

How Extra-Sensory Perception can be
used in the Investigation and Treatment
of Psychological Disorders.

by

R. CONNELL, M.D., F.R.C.P.I.

and

GERALDINE CUMMINS

First Edition
THE AQUARIAN PRESS
LONDON
1957

Atlas Occulta

ISBN: **978-1-955087-51-3**

© 2023, New World Publisher

CONTENTS

CONTENTS
(Continued)

INTRODUCTION

THE small group of Medical Cases whose histories are recorded in the following series are published in order to illustrate a method of investigation and treatment of psychological disorders that has not as yet been applied systematically for these purposes, so far as the writer is aware. The method concerns the deliberate employment of extra-sensory perception. This faculty of the mind is now recognized and accepted under the abbreviated title of E.S.P.

The method was first employed in the case of a business man, with considerable personal charm, who was faced with the prospect of loss of occupation and ruin, and his life was threatened by intermittent attacks of acute alcoholic poisoning. He had suffered from convulsions once, Delirium Tremens twice and agonizing Gastro-Dynia with collapse on more than one occasion. He had twice been placed in inebriate homes where he was treated by psychiatric specialists.

After each attack he had remained cured for a varying period and an abstainer. Each recovery was succeeded by a disheartening relapse of his malady. After the last attack, on being questioned, he confessed with great difficulty, that on certain occasions, when he never knew, he found himself quite unable to sign his own name. Fear of the disclosure of this weakness terrified him. He found that alcohol enabled him to overcome the inhibition, and for this reason he took it. His father, he stated, had suffered from the same writing inhibition.

7

It was inferred that if the cause of the writing inhibition could be discovered and explained to the patient, it might be possible to remove it, and with it the periodic alcoholism. As the writing inhibition had been present in both father and son it suggested that the cause was an inherited one, stretching back perhaps through a number of generations. It was thought in consequence that it would be both time consuming and difficult, if not impossible, to determine the cause by any of the methods of investigation in use at that time (twenty years ago).

The patient appeared to be suffering from an inherited psychosis, whose roots extended back into the past. It had not been uncovered by two specialists. It was decided by the writer to endeavour to discover the cause of the neurosis by utilizing the faculty of ESP already referred to, and if possible to apply the results to the treatment of the patient. The manner in which this investigation was carried out is recorded in a subsequent chapter. The dramatic and unexpected success which ensued, led to the application of ESP in other obscure psychological disorders from time to time, over a period of twenty years. An account of some of these cases is given, with a report of the results obtained.

A short note on ESP, and the method of its medical employment is discussed and a few conclusions are drawn. It is suggested that the history of these selected cases is adequate evidence of the value of this method of investigation and treatment, when employed judiciously, in psychological disturbances of an obscure nature, and sometimes associated with physical manifestations (*e.g.* Asthma).

Whether ESP could be employed in other types of investigation of varied nature remains to be seen. It must be borne in mind, however, that its use requires a degree of knowledge and experience that precludes its employment by those not prepared to give to its exercise both the time and thought that its proper exhibition requires. It might not be possible to employ this method to any considerable extent, owing to the difficulty of discovering and training sensitives with the necessary gifts. Time and regular practice is required to develope them.

In this series Miss Geraldine D. Cummins was employed in every case. She is well-known in this field of research, and has established a permanent reputation, by a series of remarkable publications, which demonstrate some of the uses of ESP. To her expert and highly trained mind much of the success achieved can be ascribed. The thanks of the author are also due to J. Murphy, M.D. for notes on an obscure Psycho-Neurosis that he was enabled to cure by this method.

Finally it is emphazied that it is always the primary object of a physician to cure his patient, and this object he must pursue, even if he does not fully understand the method or weapon he employs, or how it achieves its purpose. Research into these aspects are incidental. The family physician has not been engaged in proving any scientific hypothesis in regard to ESP, or in investigating the ranges of the conscious and subconscious human mind. The object has been to cure or relieve his patients. Exact scientific observation and proofs of the sensitive's findings, have not been pursued beyond the needs of the case in consequence, and any deductions made are therefore limited. With these provisos these cases are submitted.

R. CONNELL.

PUBLISHER'S NOTE : Dr. Connell, who is a well-known physician, writes under a pseudonym.

9

Chapter I

ESP OR EXTRA-SENSORY PERCEPTION

IT is necessary to submit a brief explanation of what exactly is meant by the method of investigation and treatment by the use of Extra-Sensory perception or, as it shall be referred to subsequently, ESP.

ESP can be defined as a perceptive faculty of the mind, other than those of the recognized senses of touch, sight, hearing etc.

Its existence has been believed in for a very long period in human history—investigations to prove its existence and establish its method of action have been attempted scientifically for the past seventy-five years. Only recently, in the last twenty years, has absolute proof of the existence of ESP been accepted.

This was only achieved by an enormous number of experiments confirmed and refined and repeated again and again in a number of centres in Europe and America.

The principle on which the scientific proof depends is statistical. Certain students in para-psychological laboratories guessed the sequence of symbols on a pack of cards, as they were dealt card by card. After a large number of deals it was found that certain subjects gave a correct determination of the cards dealt an infinitely greater number of times than were explained by the rules of chance.

Sometimes the successful figures were astronomical. But by setting a standard above chance as significant (ten per cent) it was found that this occurred with normal individuals, and even in the case of a disbelieving psychologist, who, when tested, was found to prove the very thesis that he himself had condemned.

The method was first employed to prove thought transference between two minds. This was named P.T. (pure telepathy). Later P.C. or pure clairvoyance or cognition was differentiated but as the two were difficult to disentangle both came to be covered by the term ESP.

It was observed that when certain apparently *unsuccessful* results were analysed carefully, the subject was found in fact to have been *the very reverse*, only that his results had indicated either a card in advance or a card behind, again with sufficient regularity to put chance out of the question. These investigations being confirmed, the terms pre-cognition (reading the future) and retro-cognition (reading the past) were added; both are covered by ESP.

Lastly a further manifestation of the unrecognised capacities of the human mind was established, when it was proved that the fall of dice could be controlled by the human mind at "a significant" level above chance.

This faculty was present even with mechanical shakers and throwers, and was termed PK or psycho-kinesis. All these different aspects of the ESP faculties of the mind are covered by the single term *psi*. It was observed that the results were not affected by distance, as good a result being obtained a hundred miles away as in the room with the experimenter. This established that ESP came under none of the known physical laws governing the transmission of information over a distance. With ESP distance made no difference. These other methods of transmitting information, are said by some physicists to diminish at the rate of half the square of the distance.

Thus was the ABC of para-psychology established and proved and reproved and passed by the mathematicians and statisticians.

It was accepted with lukewarm interest by some scientists. These did not like it because it opened up enormous fields for investigation and shook all previous conceptions.

The theory of relativity and investigations into the nature of the structure of the atom had shattered already all materially based conceptions. ESP investigations showed that that darkest corner of all, *the fundamental nature of human personality, had not been adequately understood,* and the mind had been proved to possess real and potential capacities whose existence had not been suspected.

The literature of para-psychology has become so enormous that it is quite impossible to deal with it in one short chapter. The aspect which concerns the notes that follow is covered by the terms P.C., pure cognition, and R.C., retro-cognition.

It has been known for many years that if an object belonging to an individual is submitted to an adept in ESP, that is a person who has practised and developed this faculty of the mind of which we speak, that the adept is capable of giving a very accurate account of the character of the owner, or past owner, of events in his life and past history, and even events of significance in the lives of ancestors in a similar pattern. These accounts are individual, their truth cannot always be vouched for, save by inference, or on occasion sometimes by historic research. They are not limited by time or space. If there have been several owners of the object information may be given of each.

This aspect of ESP has been named psychometry.

13

It is owing to the exercise of this aspect of ESP that the following research has been made possible. It is therefore logical to withold judgement and further reference to the subject and its range of usefulness until some of the results achieved by its exhibition in this series of cases have been considered.

Chapter II

CASE 1. A WRITING INHIBITION

THE physician in the course of his general practice is sometimes faced quite suddenly and unexpectedly with problems of extreme difficulty, and often of a highly confidential nature, associated with the maladies complained of by his patients.

It is in the region where both physical and psychological manifestations of illness are discovered to co-exist that these difficulties are often found to occur; difficulties both of diagnosis and treatment and general management which are sometimes of a most baffling character.

The following group of medical cases in some measure illustrate these difficulties. In all of them a psychological factor came to be suspected and was investigated, and the assistance received proved of vital importance in curing any physical disabilities that were also present.

Sometimes in such cases, if a psychological background is suspected, the patient himself may attach no significance to it, or he may deliberately hide a particular psychological symptom from reasons of shame or fear of disclosing it. The physician may ignore such a symptom because it is not stressed and much avoidable damage may in consequence ensue.

These general observations apply with considerable force in the first case: A case of alcoholism associated with a writing inhibition.

The previous general history, where relevant, is briefly as follows:

The case of E.F., male, aged 46 years, three children.

In 1927 his father and mother died. His mother suddenly, after a brief illness; his father after prolonged ill-health. These and other family affairs threw a very great strain on E.F.

In 1928 he was seen for the first time professionally, when he was found to be suffering from delirium tremens. He was transferred to a special home. After treatment he remained well for two years. In 1930 he was seen again for agonizing epigastric pain which was of sudden onset and had rendered him almost unconscious. He recovered after morphine followed by alkaline treatment. Careful X-ray of the stomach brought an absolutely normal report. Tentative diagnosis: spasmodic gastrodynia caused by alcohol.

Approximately five further attacks occurred at about six-monthly intervals. None were severe except the last. All except the last responded at once to alkaline treatment and a few days in bed. The last attack required three injections of morphine on three successive nights. It was then discovered that he was continuing the alcohol which had initiated the attack.

On this being quietly pointed out to him he gave up the alcohol instantly without the least apparent difficulty.

In a few days' time this point was put to him: that he must have very great strength of will to be able to give up alcohol at once—this was unusual with alcoholics—why not give it up altogether and permanently? He had proved this to be within his power again and again at least half a dozen times.

He replied: " It is not the alcohol—for it I care nothing—but I must confess that I discovered after my father's death that on certain occasions—when, I never knew—I found that I could not sign my name. An employee would bring half a dozen cheques to sign, possibly

trivial; it would not matter. I would take up my pen;
it would be impossible. At other times I could sign readily.
I never knew. A cold perspiration would burst out on me.
I would be rendered helpless and be defeated by a mere
cheque for £1. I discovered that a dose of alcohol would
overcome the inhibition.

My father told me that the same difficulty of writing
his name had overcome him in his later years. He had
given up the position of chairman because he could not
sign the minute book at the board meetings—though he
continued to direct the company. Some of his later efforts
at signature in the old minute books were grotesque. . . ."

Both father and son had found that if they anticipated
having to sign some important document in two or three
days' time the difficulty would be relatively greater.

Herein lay a partial explanation of E.F.'s capacity for
giving up alcohol at a moment's notice. The illness meant
a period without writing, under medical supervision.

He was always anxious to get back, not in order to
obtain the alcohol, but to try again, as on some occasions,
he had no difficulty in writing, and he always anticipated
absence of the inhibition. He enjoyed his business, and
had great ability for it—so long as the writing inhibition
did not interfere.

A flood of new light was thrown on the case by this
statement.

He was given advice in auto-suggestion. It was
explained to him that he was suffering from an inhibition;
an inhibition handed down to him—a race heritage, because
both he and his father had suffered from it. He was
possessed by some race-fear, due probably to a catastrophic
happening associated with writing to a distant ancestor.
That this cause was of the past, dead, finished; whatever

power it might have had at the time of its occurrence was now completely over. It had nothing to do with his own conscious mind. By auto-suggestion to his subconscious mind the day before, knowing these facts, he would completely overcome his writing inhibition from day to day, if his own suggestion were uttered with sufficient conviction. The analogous treatment of cases of " shell-shock " were explained to him, and their recovery emphasized. He was promised that further investigation of the cause would be made and that additional explanation might be found. He reported a week later after trial that the auto-suggestion proved surprisingly successful and at once.

A psychologist who was consulted suggested a partial hypnosis and a probing of the patient's subconscious mind.

This suggestion was discarded, partly owing to lack of confidence on the part of the patient's attendant, partly owing to the realization or supposition that the fear was inherited, and probably existed in his subconscious mind only as a periodic, vague, overmastering terror — the actual cause being clouded out by distance. Also he had been treated twice by psychiatrists in inebriate homes and had relapsed. A new approach was indicated.

An old family document which he possessed was borrowed with a view to probing the past of the race by means of ESP. This document conferred the freedom of the City of London on two ancestors—(1) in 1731, and (2) in 1762. It was sent to a sensitive in London, who was asked to report on it. The following record was received:

" This story will probably not be accepted. The name F— was adopted owing to persecution. It is not the race name of this family. . . . Behind this rooted disease of the mind are two forms of fear: (1) The collective fear that grew up through centuries of tribulation and (2) the fear that was generated by a terrible drama that was enacted in Spain in a past age. First I will speak of the collective fear.

These F.s were some centuries ago leaders of the Hebrew race. They came from the East to Italy and settled there about the thirteenth century. This race was high-minded, and they were always leaders of their people. This was due to their intellect and their noble origin. They felt they had to be an example to the other members of their tribe. They would not forswear their faith.

In Venice one of the first ghettos was established, and this family who lived at that time in a Venetian palace was condemned to live in one poor quarter with the other Jews. Their privileges as noblemen were taken from them. They were not permitted to serve the State as soldiers or to trade. From great riches they fell into poverty and lived in squalor. Eventually the family travelled westwards; they had connections with Spain and so went there. They lived quietly, trying not to draw attention upon themselves. They would not renounce their faith. But they always lived in fear—the terrible fear of the Inquisition. Their race name in Spain was Davila.

Pope Sixtus IV reorganized the Inquisition, and at first it was directed against Jews and Moors. They were accused of treasonable plots; but really this persecution was an attempt to secure their treasure, for it was a tradition that the Jews were wealthy.

Now because of their distinction as a family these Davilas for a time escaped notice in Spain. They had helped certain Spanish noblemen who were in monetary difficulties and were under their protection. So though fear was always their companion, they managed to live quietly in the country not far from Barcelona, where they had land.

The eldest son Juan fell in love with a woman who belonged to one of the noble houses in Spain. He was then torn by conflict because the father of the girl would only permit marriage if Juan gave up his faith—became a Spaniard, forswearing his Hebrew religion; becoming, as it was held, a traitor to his race.

Juan's father cursed him when he renounced his faith and married this Spanish lady. For a time all seemed to go well. But Juan was plunged in deep melancholy, tortured by fear of his father's curse and remorse at having appeared to be a traitor. His wife, though devoted to him, became troubled by his depression. Ultimately, when his father was ill, he saw him once more and was persuaded to give up the Catholic faith and become a Jew again, accepting his ancestors' creed. His wife's father learnt of this change and took her back to his home. She then wrote a letter to her husband entreating him to recant, threatening to kill herself if he did not return to her, by this, the only road. But now Juan was under the influence of his father and refused her request.

She wrote several times to him. After a while the letters fell into the hands of the authorities. They contained all the necessary information about Juan's family and disclosed the fact that they were people of wealth, leaders of their race, living hidden in southern Spain. It was quite enough. Every member of the family was seized, including Juan. His father died in prison; they could not keep him alive for the torture of fire. His brother and sister were burnt alive. Juan himself experienced the torture of the rack and wheel. His wife was compelled to look on at his sufferings. She had to witness his lingering agony. Up to the last it was believed that she might, through her presence, cause him to recant.

Hour after hour she had to experience the sight of his anguish. His sufferings were incredible, for he was in the prime of life—a strong, handsome man whose body was slowly broken and disfigured before her eyes.

When he was dying she perceived that his love had turned to loathing. He knew that she, through her letters had not merely betrayed himself, but all those he loved also, to horrible torture and death. So his last words were those of unspeakable hatred.

She was carrying her first child. For a time after that experience she was mad. Her son was born while she was insane. Very slowly she recovered and was living in her father's house on the east coast of Spain when news came that she was suspected of having adopted the religion of her husband. Her father was a rich man and he had enemies. So her relations decided to send Juan's wife to England with her child. She was smuggled out of the country and eventually arrived in London. She had always been devotedly attached to her husband, so her melancholy and remorse utterly destroyed the happiness of her small son as he grew up. It was given out in Spain that she was dead. She lived quietly in England, and her son adopted the name of F-.

There were queer developments in her character. She found herself unable to write, in fact she never wrote again. This neurosis extended to a fear of her son ever writing anything. She lived with an English relation who insisted that the boy should be taught to write. But for years there were conflicts in consequence. She would make passionate scenes if she ever saw the boy attempting to write. Until he was a young man he lived in fear of the rages that seized her at the sight of his writing. These scenes and also her experiences helped to develop in him a deep melancholy.   Yet he was very able and successful in business.

His grandfather supplied a little money which started him in life. But it was given on condition that his origin should be kept a close secret, because the persecution had increased in Spain and many innocent people were charged before the Inquisition. To save himself and his family the Spanish grandfather had wholly to cut himself off from young John.   So John F. became a successful merchant. His mother died when he was in the early twenties; but her experiences marred his character through bestowing on him a terrible fear, a fear that at times made it impossible for him to write his own name.   Further, he inherited the collective fear of a persecuted race. This figure of dread has accompanied his family through the centuries. It benefited him in only one way: it became a fear of losing life or the means of livelihood, so he was careful of money. In order, therefore, to secure the means of living, money-making became an obsession with him, and in old age he developed the idea that he was ruined, though he had a large fortune. This idea has been repeated in certain of his descendants. But the fear of writing anything has also come out again and again, because of that disastrous drama when his mother's letters caused the death by torture of his father and of all his father's people . . . John is the traditional christian name of the Davila family. It went from father to son for centuries . . .

These events happened between 1482 and 1492, when Torquemada was Grand Inquisitor and caused the torture of many thousands and the burning of many hundreds at the *auto-da-fé*.

This family was related in some way to the christian Bishop of Segovia.   The latter's grandfather had become converted to Christianity. But even this Christian bishop,

Arias Davila, was accused by Torquemada, and only escaped from him by fleeing to Rome and securing the support of the Pope. This bishop was well-known, but the cousins were more obscure. They remained faithful to the Jewish creed. The offence for which so many perished in Spain at that time was for the accusation of 're-judaizing,' that is to say, reconverting baptized Jews to the faith of their fathers. Old Davila did this in connection with his son, and so committed in company with his family the offence which was punished with torture and fire. The Davilas were eminent men in Spain long ago, for the Jews there were highly cultured, remarkable as physicians and administrators. The Spaniards with whom they mixed were almost barbarians.

This story contains the roots of this conflict. Such a psychological trait as this fear may be carried on down the years for centuries. A specimen of the patient's handwriting should be investigated. The case could then be examined in greater detail and treatment discussed. The link with the living patient is needed to see how far he has inherited this tragic bequest of the Inquisition."

This document was read to the patient. The manner in which it was obtained was explained to him in a way he could comprehend.

It was emphasized that this history, the true cause of his writing inhibition, was in the past—dead—could exercise no power over him, that in future he would be able to sign anything without a stimulant by realizing this history, which was undoubtedly true. That he had a high family and race tradition to maintain; and, as the head of the family, it must be his ambition to become the chairman and leader of the firm his ancestors had guided and built up.

On May 15th, 1935, the sensitive obtained a further statement concerning the parchment. A letter written by the patient was also examined on this occasion. The following record was received:

" (1) This parchment should be preserved. It is entirely beneficial, for it aroused in its past owners a feeling of pride and courage. These feelings helped the people of an older generation to fight their fears. There are indeed only good memories about the parchment.

(2) The man who wrote this letter has an excellent brain and he has an inherited gift for making sound decisions in connection with his business, but he is highly strung and sensitive, resembling the Spanish woman who was the ancestor, and also her son John.

Their fears were transmitted in the race memory and these he has inherited.

He should be told this hidden history of his family. The reason he cannot write at times is due to the letters written by an ancestor who betrayed her husband and his family. Added to that is another fear. This man respected and loved his father. When he learnt of his father's incapacity at times to write his name it came as a shock to his mind. It roused the dormant race-fear, which came to control him at intervals.

He should be told that each individual inherits not merely physical characteristics but a race-memory from their forebears which is buried in their unconscious mind. His incapacity to sign his name being simply due to the inherited unconscious memory of a race-terror. He can conquer it entirely by realizing its origin, by realizing also that it is partly due to his learning that the man he revered suffered in this way also.

One exercise that is sometimes useful, and should be so in this case, is for him to say to himself before he falls

24

asleep, ' I am perfectly able to write. I shall sign those cheques tomorrow at the office with perfect ease.'

The subconscious as a rule is sensitive to suggestion just before a man falls asleep. These suggestive statements can be phrased according to the nature of the work or writing the man has to deal with.

This man is master in his own house—the house of the conscious and unconscious mind—he has but to exert his authority fearlessly in this way and he is bound to overcome the inhibition of being unable to write, that is if he does so knowing the race history that gave rise to the fear.

In telling him this history you may more easily explain how it was obtained if you take the analogy of the voice being preserved in wireless waves. Equally, memories are preserved on another wave-length: for strong emotional thoughts give out a certain electrical force that is recorded on waves in the ether. These vibrations do not perish. These memory vibrations hang about this parchment because its first owner knew the family history in Spain and Italy. So it was picked up as a wireless receiver picks up sound vibrations.

This man should also be encouraged to have a belief in himself. Instil into his mind a feeling of pride in being the head of an old and very able race with a fine record of achievement which he, because of his ability, is perfectly able to continue.

This man may in the future be visited, as in the past, with fits of melancholy derived from the old collective race fear induced by persecution, and from the Spanish history. This might lead, and has led him, to try and escape by means of some exciting stimulant. This fact must be borne in mind.''

This communication was read to the patient. It confirmed and greatly amplified the teaching of auto-suggestion already given, and further gave him increased confidence in his medical attendant.

In presence of the medical attendant a further investigation was made before the parchment was returned, and with the following result:

"There is a secondary cause in connection with the psychological malady of the F.s. One of the ancestors of the patient, Frederic by name, appears to have married a Miss Pushe. Now the psychological fears inherited from that terrible Spanish drama from the mother of the first John F. would in two hundred years have lost some of their power over the F.s' subconscious mind. But at the time they were beginning to fade they were greatly strengthened owing to the addition brought to them by Miss Pushe, who became Mrs. F. In his youth the father of Miss Pushe was fighting with a boy on the edge of a river. It seems that, entirely by accident, he pushed the schoolboy into the water. The latter was drowned. Pushe, who had then another name, was in despair. He was quite unable to write his own name in consequence, and he never wrote it again, but had it changed by law to 'Pushe.' He died through an accident when his daughter, who became Mrs. F., was about twelve years of age. Actually she had no real psychological difficulties, but she brought to the race memory of the F.s what might be described as another attack upon the weak point—their feeling of remorse and their inhibitions as regards writing their name.

This is the secondary cause, though the original trouble in Spain went far deeper, but it gained a much stronger hold on the F.s through the second misfortune, and prevented it from becoming weaker through the passage of time."

A combined copy of the records was given to the patient. Only the account of the reinforcement of the inhibition was omitted. It was thought better to leave the one clear-cut cause to act "alone" in his mind.

He was given a photograph of the parchment from which the script was obtained in order to emphasize in his mind the value it bore to himself and his family, and also a copy of some historic evidence that has since been collected in order to reinforce his belief in the truth of the document.

In reviewing this case it is necessary to assess the evidential value of the information obtained by means of ESP, as far as is possible, and refer to the character of the patient and the result of treatment. The strange story of the boy who changed his name to Pushe has been verified by family records. It was quite unknown to the sensitive. A rough family tree is submitted and the following points noted:

According to the sensitive's record, the first member of the family to appear in London was John F., the son of the Spanish lady. Date 1490-1500.

No record of the family is known for two centuries until John F., who obtained the freedom of the City of London in 1731, the son of Robert F. Though a gap of about one-hundred and fifty years is present, one cannot fail to note the persistence of the name John. Stated to be the family name of the Davilas, also that John is a Hebrew name, and that the F.s are found living in London.

The family remained in London (city-dwellers and apparently merchants) until 1780, when one Robert came to X.

Two branches of the family remained in X, both descended from Frederic, who married Miss Pushe.

Of the two branches of the family, only those known to the medical attendant are mentioned. All subsequent to R.C.F. and D.F. were personally known to him, and most of them consulted him professionally from time to time in the last twenty years. It will be observed that the writing inhibitions (w) has occurred five times to his personal knowledge in one branch. It may have occurred more often without his knowledge. He has heard of four more cases of writing difficulties in relatives since, one of whom is the eldest son of the patient, who had a fine record during the last war, in the navy, and is now a director of the firm, he confessed his weakness diffidently to the author recently and is receiving treatment. The delusional insanity—with the delusion of loss of money and consequent injury to their family—has occurred four times in the other branch as far as is known. (1) Insanity with suicide two cases, (2) insanity without suicide, (3) two attempts at suicide have been observed in other members.

It is significant that the sensitive, without knowledge of these facts, yet described the actual nature of the delusion from which certain members of the family were said to have suffered. This proved identical with that from which three members in three generations are known to have suffered; the medical attendant being in personal charge of two.

Points, some of which cannot be marked on the family tree:

(1) A very marked neurasthenic tendency associated with unreasoning and excessive fear of loss of health; very noticeable to a family physician and common amongst people of Jewish origin.

(2) Considerable (above the average) business capacity in a fair proportion.

(a) The patient is a highly strung type. A good athlete with considerable physical courage.

He recovered completely from the writing inhibition.

He found it more difficult to overcome the periodic alcoholic tendency, but after two relapses, he has remained completely free for fifteen years.

He has become Chairman of the Company, and additional responsibilities, etc., make relapse out of the question.

(3) A very marked Hebraic countenance with sallow complexion and hooked, rather broad nose and thick lips, appearing again and again both in family portraits and in living members.   (h)

(The persistence of the Hebraic appearance can be explained on the assumption that it became a dominant genetic factor, during thousands of years of Jewish inter-marriage, prior to 1480, when they left Spain, became Christians, and intermarried only with Christians, for four hundred years (twelve generations?).

(4) A high resistance to most bacteriological infections —such as might be expected in city dwellers.

(5) A marked melancholic tendency is very noticeable.

(6) As a family they are in no way lacking in physical courage.

(7) An asthmatic tendency is marked.   (a)

These different points are most convincing as evidence of the truth of the sensitive's record.

Further evidence collected at a later date from historic records is here given after the family tree.

FAMILY TREE

Spanish Record
(obtained by
Psychometry)

John Davila (died in prison)—Arias Davila, Bishop o
Segovia (a cousin)

Juan   Brother   Sister
(died by torture)   (burnt alive)   (burnt alive)

First Appearance
of Neurosis

John F. fled to London with his mother about 1500.

In London
(obtained from
family records)

Gap of 150 years. (Great Plague and Fire of London
1666.
Robert F. (probably born about 1680).

John F. (in 1731 became freeman of City of London)

John F. (in 1762   ,,   ,,   ,,   ,,   )

Robert F. left London for X—.

Reinforcement
of Neurosis

Frederic F., born 1779, married Miss Pushe.

R.F.   D.F. (i) (s)

R.C.F.(a) H.(h) E.(h)   F.(i, h) W.(h) D.(h) R.(h) J.(h) M

A.(h) R.(w, h) J.(w, a, h) G. K.(a, h) C.(h) F. N. N.
                            | (h) (h) (h)
(All known per-   (h)   (w)
sonally by Medi-   (a)
cal Attendant)

E.F.(w) (patient)   H. E. (h, s) E. (attempted s

C. (w) G.(h) R.(a, h)

NOTE.—In the above Tree the abbreviations are as under :
    (w)   writing inhibition or neurosis.   (a)   asthmatical tendency.
    (h)   Hebraic appearance.   (s)   suicide.
    (i)   insanity (with delusion of loss of money).

NOTE.

SOME PROVED HISTORIC FACTS THAT HAVE SINCE BEEN COLLECTED

Persecution of the Jews in Venice

A census taken in 1152 showed one thousand, three hundred Jews in Venice. An event which probably greatly increased the number of Jews in Venice was the conquest of Constantinople by the Venetians and French in 1204. They went to Venice for business and some remained there.

The right of the Jews to reside in Venice always remained precarious. In 1394 they were banished, but business, especially banking, became so disorganised that they were recalled within a year.

In 1423 all Jews of Venice were forbidden to hold real estate or to engage in certain trades. Other repressive measures followed.

Venice was one of the first cities to establish a ghetto.

The Inquisition in Spain

During the cruel persecution of 1391 many thousands of Jewish families accepted baptism to save their lives. Of these, many were only outward converts and continued secretly the practices of their faith.

In 1478 Isabella was prevailed on by her husband Ferdinand to appeal to Pope Sixtus IV for a bill to reinstitute the Inquisition into Castile. This was granted.

She resolved upon the forcible conversion of the Jews. The latter had married freely into Christian families, including some of the oldest and most distinguished in Spain. Therefore the property held by the Jews and those families " tainted " by Jewish blood was considerable and formed the real reason for the virulence of their persecution. Most stringent of all were the measures taken against those

accused of "re-judaizing," and, in spite of promises of forgiveness to those who confessed, such " confessions " were
met with death by torture and fire.

In Castile the Inquisition was formally proclaimed on
January 2nd, 1481. On February 6th, 1481, six men and
women were burned at the stake at Seville.

On October 17th, 1483, Thomas de Torquemada, then
sixty-three years of age, and prior of a monastery at
Segovia, his native city, was appointed the first Inquisator-
General. He held the position for fifteen years, i.e., from
1483 to 1498, when he died. During that period about
two thousand, two hundred persons were burned alive,
while about seventeen thousand saved their lives by giving
up their property and submitting to lesser penalties, such
as civil incapacity, imprisonment and banishment.

The Catalonian cities stubbornly opposed the Inquisition and in 1486 there were riots at Teruel, Barcelona and
Valencia.

In 1487 Torquemada appointed Alfonso de Espina
Inquisitor of Barcelona. De Espina began his activities
on January 25th, 1488.

Among the names of the victims given there is no
mention of Davila; the names are chiefly those belonging
to distinguished—and wealthy—Spanish families; very few
names are mentioned, but there are many examples quoted
closely resembling the story given.

Juan Arias Davila

Torquemada accused even bishops who were of Jewish
descent, among them being Juan Arias Davila, Bishop of
Segovia. His immediate family history is as follows:

Diego Arias Davila, Minister of Henry IV of Castile,
was born of Jewish parents in Segovia and died in 1466.
He and his family embraced the Christian faith. He rose

to great power and influence and became the farmer and administrator of the royal taxes.

His eldest son, Pedro Davila, married Donna Maria de Mendoza, niece of the First Duke de Infantado and a grandchild of Marquis de Santillana.

His second son, Juan Arias Davila, became Bishop of Segovia. Full of hatred against the Jews, he caused sixteen of them, who had been accused of a ritual murder, to be burned at the stake. In spite of his zeal, he was accused by Torquemada that his grandfather had "rejudaized." Only by a personal visit to the Pope did he escape ruin from the Inquisition.

Torquemada and Bishop Arias Davila were both of Segovia, and the former would have known of the Jewish origin of the latter.

Pope Sixtus IV was named Francesco della Rovere, and was born in 1414. He was Pope from A.D. 1471-1484.

None of the details of these historical records were known to the medical attendant or to the sensitive at the time that the family document was investigated. They were recovered after considerable investigation in the British Museum and elsewhere at a later date. A full account of them and of Bishop Arias Davila's escape from the Inquisition can be found in *Torquemada and the Spanish Inquisition*, by Rafael Sabatini.

It is suggested that the fact that the history of Arias Davila as recorded by the sensitive has been proved true, and taken in conjunction with the other historic records, is confirmation of the whole of the remainder of the story. The patient himself accepted it as true and he now enjoys good health and is in full activity.

c

CASE II. A CASE OF PERIODIC SELF-IMPOSED FASTING

IN the subsequent cases the use of the same method of investigation and treatment is demonstrated. In none of them, however, has any close enquiry been made to verify the information obtained by ESP. The patients in most cases accepted its findings as if they had already known them to be true.

The reason that this course is adopted is partly owing to the great difficulty met with, and to the time consumed in pursuing such research; time that should be spent in treating the patient. Further, personal enquiries as to the actuality of the information which is being utilized creates loss of confidence and doubt in the mind of the patient, which militates against the cure of his psychological ailment. He must be informed categorically that such and such is the definite, absolute cause of his illness, even if an unexpected revelation to him. Every minutest suggestion of doubt must be eliminated if success is to be achieved.

The patient was a spinster aged fifty years. On consultation she was emaciated, extremely pallid and utterly exhausted physically, to the extent that even speaking seemed to be an effort.

She stated that she had lost all appetite for food for the past six weeks and had been prevented by her feeling of sickness from eating anything. She had suffered from previous similar attacks, from which she recovered. After a superficial examination which disclosed nothing further it was decided to admit her to hospital at once, owing to her extreme prostration, for fuller investigation.

34

No further cause for her illness and collapsed condition was determined. All her organs appeared normal. No chronic focus of infection was present. No evidence of cancer could be discovered. No pigmentation or other suggestion of adrenalin deficiency was found. Suspicion of any obscure blood condition was eliminated. Except for a minor degree of secondary anæmia, which rapidly resolved, no deviation from normal health could be observed.

She was treated with liver extract, iron, stimulants, and tonics. She recommenced taking food, with appetite, shortly after admission to hospital, and in a matter of three weeks appeared to be completely restored to health; increase in weight, fourteen pounds.

On cross-examination she stated that the attacks had been recurring for twenty years, since the death of her mother from consumption. That latterly they were lasting for longer periods of time, and recovery of strength took longer, and that quite suddenly she would lose all desire for food and would eat nothing. This would continue for about six weeks. Equally suddenly, sometimes in the middle of the night, an irrestible craving for food would replace the loss of appetite. No cause for the loss of desire for food could be determined.

It was thought that the periodicity of the attacks might be associated with abnormality in the sexual cycle. A course of ovarian therapy was administered before she was sent home in good health.

She reported two months later that she had passed through another severe attack at home and was now recovering. She had lost only four pounds in weight when she reported and appeared in fair health.

One other point associated with her history concerns her brother. He served in the First World War. Two years previous to her consultation he suffered from sudden hæmoptysis. He lost over three pints of blood. He recovered from the hæmorrhage, and after six months at a sanatorium also recovered from the tubercular infection from which he was suffering. He has since married and is at work again in good health. One other brother and sister enjoy good health.

This is a type of case which is extremely difficult to deal with in general practice. The patient was suffering from unexplained attacks of loss of appetite and starvation of about six weeks' duration, producing a condition of almost complete exhaustion, followed by unexplained recovery. No physical cause was discoverable.

These attacks had been continuing from 1924 for sixteen years. The basis of the condition appeared to be some obscure, unexplained neurosis. Unless some cause of this suppostitious neurosis was discovered no form of psychological treatment could be initiated with either any confidence or any great prospect of success.

A general practitioner has neither the time nor the experience and patience necessary to probe a patient's mind by psycho-analysis or by hypnosis. And it is questionable if a cause for the neurosis could have been elaborated by these means, in this case, by an expert in such methods. Search amongst obscure symptoms and physical indications had proved quite inefficacious. Further, the patient lived at a great distance.

Alternative treatment, by recommending change of air, and administering bromide and valerian, would be a confession of failure.

It was essential to discover the cause of the supposed neurosis. An explanation of what was contemplated was

made to the patient, and a ring which she was wearing
was, with her consent, despatched to the sensitive in
London. An account of the patient's physical symptoms
was written in a letter to the sensitive and she was asked
to investigate the psychological background.

This is the reply that was received:—

"There is graven on this ring a definite fear. The
woman to whom it belongs is a very interesting character.
She has naturally a lively, attractive disposition, but she
has inherited from her forebears an up-and-down temperament. She is capable of moods of great optimism and of
moods of deep pessimism; this disposition often accom-
panies a tendency to phthisis. An individual dying of
phthisis will often, for instance, believe that he is going to
get well, is subject to moods of deep despondency and great
optimism. This kind of temperament left the patient open
to a fear that seems to have been imparted to her at the
very outset of life.

Her mother was a delicate woman. For years she did
not let others know of her feeling of physical weakness.
But it was quite pronounced, yet she stood up to it as best
she could. Now during the nine months of pregnancy,
if a mother is a prey to any very strong emotions, these
emotions will influence the subconsciousness of the baby
in her womb.

Feeling very weak and low in herself, the mother of
the woman who owned this ring was afraid from the time
she conceived her. The fear was that in bringing forth this
life she herself would die, or even if she survived she would
be so delicate she could do very little for her precious baby.
The mother suppressed this fear so far as she could and
hid it from others. So it became stronger by reason of
this struggle to suppress it. It sowed the seed of a fear

of life in the baby's subconsciousness, for it was associated with the bringing forth of life which threatened, according to the mother's belief, to lead to her own death. This seed lay dormant in the child's unconscious mind for many years. If she had had a dull, even temperament it would never have affected her, but being sensitive and inclined to be up and down in moods she eventually became strongly influenced by it. Her mother's last illness and death gave it force, led it to grow into a complex. It became what it was originally, a fear of life through the menace of death. Affection for her mother, the sight of her ill and slowly dying, then her death, worked unconsciously on this sensitive daughter's mind.

Mentally the daughter is perfectly sound and rational. This irrational fear is really not her fault. It is due to the unfortunate fears of her mother during the nine months the baby was so closely associated with her emotions. But the daughter's fear of life after the mother's death took the form of fasting, of a loathing of food. When this fear is uppermost it completely overcomes the instinct of self-preservation and she eats nothing. This fear is planted in the subconscious mind of the patient, so she is *consciously unaware* of it, though she is the victim of its effects. There have been other minor influences which have helped to keep it alive, such as anxiety about her brother when at the war, and later anxiety about his health. If the doctor thinks she is capable of understanding what is at the root of her trouble he could tell her of it and explain how, knowing it, she can now overcome it. That in future she will never again want to go off food, for doing so is simply giving way to an emotion of a bygone time which is completely irrational and without foundation. It belongs to the past and the far past, is finished with, ended.

On the other hand, the doctor must realize that this complex has *intimate sexual associations* with the mother's womb, the desire to escape back into it, where there is no need to eat. The complex is therefore related to intimate sexual life, so must be dealt with with more than ordinary care and, of course, if not thought advisable, not disclosed to the patient. Such a patient, if at the change of life, is naturally more inclined to be the prey of fancy and fantasy, of nerves and emotional life.

There is another course that may be taken with or without the explanation of the complex. The patient customarily has eaten rather devitaminized foods; a sound *unconscious instinct* warns her against the home diet. The instinct being unthinking merely adds considerably to her feeling of repugnance at times to all food. She could be told with advantage that one cause of her eating nothing for certain periods was due to this instinct. The doctor knows the proper foods. He should give her a list of them.

To sum up: the two causes of this determination not to take food at intervals are (1) the fear acquired before birth, and (2) the instinctive but quite wholesome objection to devitaminized foods.''

The patient is naturally of an affectionate, kindly nature, and the benefit to others through her keeping fit by eating regularly might be mentioned.''

By utilizing this material supplied by means of ESP the difficulty of dealing with the psychological aspects of this case were lessened.

The explanation of the complex was given to the patient, and the greater part of the communication read to her.

It was emphasized that the complex had been imposed on her by causes out of the past which had long since terminated. That their effect had finished. That she could overcome all inclination to fast by means of this knowledge, and by dismissing to the background of her mind all thoughts of illness and unhappiness because their cause was removed.

That her duty was clear: she was to continue to benefit others by her affectionate and lively personality.

She was to follow definite rules with regard to diet and rational, healthy living.

That the loathing of food would never again recur or overcome her.

This instruction, amplified, formed the basis of her psychological treatment.

In the last six months she has both written and called personally to express her thanks, she has increased a further stone in weight, and states she enjoys perfect health, and has had no further illness.

A close investigation disclosed the fact that the patient had nursed her mother during her terminal illness—phthisis.

(It may be noted that by exercising ESP the sensitive recorded the subjoined ascertainable facts, which were quite outside of her knowledge, and were not conveyed to her, perfectly correctly:

  (1) A uniquely accurate estimate of the patient's character and temperament.
  (2) The death of the mother by phthisis (as is implied).
  (3) The illness and war service of the brother.
  (4) The time of life of the patient.
  (5) An analysis of the neurosis and its suppositious causes of a profoundly apposite nature, scientifically satisfying, and eminently suitable for psychological utilization.).

Fifteen years have passed since this report was written. The patient lives in an isolated place. Owing to transport difficulties, imposed by war stringency, etc., it was impossible for her to consult her physician.

He has learnt through her relatives and by letters that though she has never gone on "hunger strike" since her treatment, she has retired to her room owing to a fancied dislike to her brother-in-law, with whom she lives. She is perfectly happy and otherwise normal, but evidently uses him as a psychological barrier to prevent contact with the world and life which she still fears. Further treatment is rendered impossible at present.

CASES III, IV, V, VI. FOUR CASES OF CLAUSTROPHOBIA

THE four following cases presented symptoms of dizziness associated with fear.

The first case, a lady of twenty-five years, stated that when the dizziness occurred it was accompanied by "a terrible feeling." The attacks of dizziness occurred only in enclosed places and particularly small rooms. Her family history was to some extent known; she was one of a family of thirteen. Two brothers suffered from diabetes. They were all engaged in extensive farming operations, and her family had been known to have been employed at this occupation for at least several generations.

The patient was of a gentle, timid disposition, of rather poor physical development and of a somewhat worn appearance. No physical disability was determined, and her case was therefore investigated.

The following report was received from an examination of a specimen of her handwriting sent to London:

"The writer of this letter is highly strung and sensitive. She comes of a good family and her ancestors in some cases had remarkable qualities. But two or three of them lived hard. This led to the stock becoming rather exhausted and to a sensitive nervous system in this generation.

There is certainly a tendency here to claustrophobia and there are other fears latent in this woman's subconscious mind. She has inherited from her people, who were gentlefolk, a certain timidity due to the fact that some of them lived in the country a rather isolated life. But the fundamental cause of this lady's fear when in a confined space may be traced back perhaps two-hundred years. One of her ancestors, possibly on the mother's side, owned a house and land in the country. This man was a fine character in his own way. But it seems that during troubled times a band of wild men—either tenants or people who came from the hills—one night broke suddenly into this man's house and set it alight. The wife of the owner of the house was in the first months of carrying a child. Only with difficulty did she make her escape. Indeed, she was caught in a small room that rapidly filled with smoke. She awoke to the smell of burning and to the shouts of rough men. Terrified, she perceived the smoke creeping about the room, becoming thicker and thicker. She got up and tried to reach the door. Great waves of smoke came in. Half suffocated, she struggled forward to the threshold, where she collapsed in a faint on the floor.

Her husband, at the risk of his life, rescued her, and after a while she revived in the cold night air. But she caught pneumonia from exposure in that bitter night, and during her delirium kept seeing the images of that room filling up with smoke, and went through again and again in her fever the agony of terror experienced in those few minutes. Slowly she recovered her health. But the fear of being shut up and trapped in a small room was, during that period of illness, transmitted to the child she was carrying.

Her experience in that fire became a part of the race-memory of that family. When the incident of the burning of the house in that lonely countryside was forgotten consciously by the descendants of this unfortunate woman it still remained as a well-marked recollection engraven on the unconscious mind of the race. Some of the family were not affected by it, others less robust developed certain weaknesses of a nervous character.

Physically the patient whose handwriting I am sensing is still rather run down. She ought to get out into the open air, take plenty of regular exercise and find an interest or interests of an absorbing character.

As it occurred such a long time ago and has not been strengthened since by similar terrible shocks to her direct ancestors, it is not a pronounced thing. It has therefore no great hold. She ought to say aloud to herself at night just before she falls asleep, ' My mind is the ruler of my body. Nothing can make me afraid. I am at peace and happy in any small room or confined space.'

The original cause of her fear—that shock to her ancestor when she was in a delicate condition—has no power over the patient when she is really physically fit and has some interesting and absorbing occupation for her mind.

Try also to instil into Miss J. more confidence, more belief in herself. She is too diffident and distrusts her own powers.

43

Let her try to assert herself and believe in herself, for she has plenty of innate capacity and intelligence. But lack of confidence, which is clearly a fault in her, greatly hinders her in life.

Do not tell the patient the following. There is a decidedly unstable heredity, so a cure will probably take a little time and her medical attendant must watch her, and be careful lest nervous symptoms of another character break out. On the other hand, if she faithfully follows his directions heredity should be conquered."

CASE IV

THE second case of dizziness occurred in a lady, a chemist's assistant, aged twenty-four years. She had noticed the dizziness for about a year. She had been sent away for a change of air and holiday, and later had been treated with bromide and valerian; neither treatment had benefited her. Her attacks occurred both in the open air and in closed spaces. They were very frightening because of the fear of falling. On the last occasion when an attack occurred in the street she had to be supported into a shop, where she rested for half an hour before returning home. She had to give up her occupation.

Physical examination, including sight and hearing, yielded no information. Slight dysmenorrhoea was present and was treated with benefit by ovarian substance. The attacks of dizziness and fear remained, and as no cause could be discovered her case was investigated by ESP.

The following report was received from an examination of a specimen of her handwriting sent to London:

" I feel in this handwriting a young and very sensitive girl. She seems to be rather run down, just a little below par and no more than that.

44

I feel, however, that a centre of balance in her brain does not always function absolutely instantaneously with the mind. This would not affect her balance (so very slight is this weakness) if it were not that her nervous system is easily stimulated by her subconscious mind.

The subconscious is aware of the slight, very occasional slow co-ordination between the centre for balance and the mind, and is afraid therefore of her falling. It has conveyed this self-preservation fear with some force to the consciousness, which indeed is now haunted by what is really an unreasoning fear. For there is no danger of this girl falling because of this slight weakness, which in any case is only a little apparent at the time or beginning of the monthly period. The girl is neither neurotic nor hysterical and her brain is perfectly normal. All that is actually physically wrong is a slightly slow functioning of the centre for balance just about the time of the period. She ought at that time to take things fairly easily for a day or two. She should also lead for a time a healthy outdoor life and try to take plenty of exercise and fresh air.

I recommend a special form of exercise she could do in her own room or anywhere private in which she bends her legs up and down and also, if she can bring herself to do it, rise up and down on her toes—and first hold on to something if the fear of falling or staggering takes possession of her. Secondly, she should be told there is no trouble in her brain to cause her to be afraid. That the fear is due merely to the unreasoning subconscious mind being quite wrongly alarmed lest she might fall because her centre of balance in the brain is occasionally a little slow in co-ordinating with the rest.

But that she has actually quite a sufficient sense of balance to keep her walking or running in an erect position without difficulty. There was an added cause in her being

45

in the chemist's place of business for a short time. The subconscious became afraid there in the enclosed place where she was for a number of hours. The enclosed place roused the dormant fear which is allied to claustrophobia in this particular symptom.

I think the patient should not be given a sedative but should, on the contrary, be stimulated by a good tonic. It is necessary to make her physically as well and strong as possible. For then the health of the body will help to overcome the unreasoning and really unfounded fear of the mind. But she is definitely a normal and intelligent person and can herself overcome the terror if she will relax completely and say aloud to herself that owing to better health she has nothing to fear any more. This remark said aloud when the speaker is resting and drowsy is undoubtedly helpful.

I must add—though don't tell her so—that she has a weak will and must be given confidence in herself. The will has easily and quickly surrendered where it would not do so in a strong character."

The psychological treatment carried out in both these cases was similar.

A considerable portion of their reports was read to the patients in each case. The respective causes of their conditions were pointed out to them, and the method of overcoming them was emphasized.

The first case reported prompt improvement, and in two years' time, when the physician was calling about another matter, she said on being questioned that though she still noticed the dizziness on occasions in confined spaces, it never frightened her or worried her in any way. She has since married and gone to Canada. The chemist's assistant returned to work almost at once and has continued at it. She is satisfied of her recovery.

In these cases the sensitive determined:

(1) The nature of the neuroses.

(2) Gave an accurate account of both patients' characters and temperaments.

(3) Indicated the farming occupation of the first patient's family.

(4) Gave suppositious causes for the neuroses, differing entirely in nature in both cases. These causes were explanatory and of a sufficiently convincing nature to enable the patients to overcome the incapacitating part of their ailments when utilized with judgment by their medical attendant.

CASE V. A CASE OF MILD CLAUSTROPHOBIA

THIS case is recorded because it illustrates a point referred to in a later chapter dealing with ESP: the insulating property of glass.

A young girl of seventeen was sent for consultation by her mother. It was much against her own inclination and wishes; she stated she was afraid to go near a doctor. She related that the reason for the consultation was as follows:

In the last three months, on three separate occasions, once in church, twice in a cinema, she had experienced a sensation of dizziness; she noticed palpitation and she had to leave the buildings because of fear of unconsciousness. In each case, as soon as she reached the open air she recovered at once, completely. The cinemas were slightly stuffy. The church was cold and well ventilated.

She was carefully examined physically; she was told with emphasis that all her organs were perfect. She was given a mixture and left the consulting-room completely reassured of her recovery. It was a case that required no

47

elaborate investigation or treatment. However, a specimen of her handwriting was obtained and submitted, enclosed in a glass photograph frame, to the sensitive. She placed her left hand on the glass, and, shutting her eyes, after half a minute her right hand wrote:

"It is very difficult; I make no contact; there is an emptiness about it."

After half a minute the glass was removed. The left hand now directly contacted the writing. Again after half a minute her right hand wrote rapidly:

"This is the writing of a woman of a bright disposition. She seems to be rather tired and run down. I think she suffers from a fear of crowds or being shut in.

There is a lurking sensitiveness in the writing's atmosphere. Now I sense a shock in early childhood. It seems as if she was shut in somewhere, either locked into a room or enclosed space by accident by herself, or she was shut up somewhere for punishment. At any rate she became, when very young, terrified, because for a short time she was shut up by herself. This is the cause, partly of a slight nervous condition or fear, at present. There seems also to be a physical condition. She needs some building up. She will respond to treatment, diet and fresh air. It seems as if she comes from a highly sensitive family and this time she was shut up is associated with a race memory. That is why it has a certain force.

An ancestor of hers was taken prisoner in a war. I think it happened long ago, but he suffered terribly during this imprisonment and was very ill when released. His experience left a definite mark on the race-consciousness. The fact that these two memories, one personal, one racial, are not in her conscious memory probably would lead to their having greater influence on her. But it seems as if she is only a very mild case and that she is intelligent and sensible, so is likely to become perfectly well shortly."

This experiment was carried out simply to illustrate the inhibiting effect of a sheet of glass on the sensitive's ability to interpret.

The patient has since been interviewed and has recovered. It was not found necessary to utilize the information obtained to reinforce her confidence in herself.

CASE VI. THE YOUNG PHYSICIAN

AS the causes that originate attacks of claustrophobia are often obscure and difficult to unravel, and as the condition is perhaps more common than is realized generally, a further example is recorded with the result of its investigation by E.S.P.

The case was that of a brilliant young physician. At a medical meeting he happened to mention to the author that he had suffered severely from claustrophobia in the past. That he had had to leave cinemas, places of entertainment, etc., frequently. He considered that he had to a large degree overcome this fear. He attributes it to two experiences of childhood. (1) When he was playing with a number of small boys a large wooden box or pen was placed in turn on top of one or other of their number, completely covering him. When he became the victim himself he was terrified into a frenzy by the darkness and the confined space. (2) Later he noticed a particular horror. It was when he passed through a tall, narrow, built-in lane into which an atmosphere of steam and smell used on occasions to issue from a bakery that stood near its centre.

It was pointed out to him that as he was the only one among the party of small boys who later developed

49

claustrophobia there were probably other factors associated with this neurosis.

His abnormal reaction to steam and smell in the narrow street rather suggested an experience with fire and smoke, possibly to an ancestor. The matter could be investigated. The physician was interested, and suggested that this should be done.

It was agreed that the sensitive should be given the information that the patient was a physician who had recovered more or less completely from claustrophobia, but that his psychological background in this connection was sought for further confirmation.

His fountain pen was utilized for this research and the subjoined record was obtained:

" The owner of this pen is extremely able. He has a quick clear brain, it darts here and there, almost unconsciously picking up the salient points in a problem and arriving rapidly at a conclusion. He would be excellent at research or in some special line of work because he has, as well as a clever brain, imaginative powers. But he has to pay for this in being rather highly strung and in having acute sensitiveness, which he conceals as far as possible. This sensitiveness makes him inclined to be cautious, where actions are concerned, in regard to his personal life. He might miss chances in this way through remaining at the same work too long.

Yet in the field of thought he is adventurous when he chooses. He is an interesting character, but though apparently open and frank he has a certain subconscious caution which is a racial inheritance. So he is not inclined to seek great intimacy with people. He can go a certain way with them and then withdraws into himself. Some way back in the racial history his family were people owning

a considerable amount of land, they were innately aristocratic but lived in a time when they were on the wrong side.
They were rebels against the existing order of things, their
religion was penalized, so they lived under great nervous
strain. This bred in them the cautious, rather chronically
anxious type of mind. Their lands were stolen from them,
several of them fought and lost, they were hunted and in
hiding, two of them served long terms of imprisonment
as suspected rebels. One, a direct ancestor, after about
fifteen years of a horrible confinement, in which he was
half starved and ill-treated, emerged from the prison almost
completely broken nervously. He never recovered mentally
from this incarceration. He did not go mad, but lost all
initiative, was haunted by the horrible memory of the tiny
prison cell in which he had lived in filth and rags for fifteen
years.

Later in life he married and had a son. Vividly on
his mind was imprinted the fear of a small confined space.
That picture was passed on to his son's subconsciousness.
Night after night his son, as a small boy, used to see his
father, while still asleep, leap from his bed and beat on
the walls of the room while he screamed: '' Let me out !
For God's sake, let me out ! '' The boy was an orphan,
his mother having died, and he slept in the same room
as his father. Too young to understand that his father
was only in sleep dreaming of a past horrible experience,
the small boy inherited the same unreasoning dread of a
confined space. He passed on this memory picture to his
descendants. It might have faded in time or become
indefinite in the race memory, but one descendant was
trapped in his bedroom at night when the house caught
fire; the stairs were burning, I think, at any rate for a brief
while, death by fire seemed certain. He seems to have
escaped by the window, his injuries were serious. Though

he recovered he never forgot the terror of that time, and this fear revivified the old complex. He would not speak of that experience to anyone, and that repression nourished the racial fear. These events happened a long time ago.

The owner of this pen, when very young, was locked into a small room, possibly for punishment. When darkness fell he became very frightened, and the fear linked him up with the ancestral fantasy. He had probably forgotten this episode. There was also another experience in his life, which is not at the moment clear to me, that intensified it, and, like the striking of a match, produced the light that led to the explosion of the complex in claustrophobia.

This man, however, is eminently sane, and his quick intelligence and reasoning mind will master this complaint, if he experiences that feeling at any time.''

In due course this psychological background was submitted to the physician, and the following information bearing on it is added.

It is to be noticed in the first instance:

(1) That the sensitive was unusually impressed by the evidence of a high degree of ability shown by the physician. It is the case that the character of the individual whose object is being investigated by this method is always first described by this sensitive.

In this case the author himself had been impressed similarly by the clarity, speed and comprehensiveness of the physician's mental reactions and judgments.

He had taken part as an assistant examiner in both his M.B. and M.D. examinations; he was therefore in a position that justified the forming of such an opinion.

(2) The physician stated that twice he had had an opportunity of carrying out research. Once he had been

selected for a research post in physiology when still a student. Once, on obtaining his M.B. degree, he had been offered a Rockfeller research scholarship. He failed to take up either of these posts, partly owing to family reasons, partly, as he admitted, owing to his own dilatoriness in coming to a decision. This trait in the physician is emphasized by the sensitive in her impression of his character. Moreover, she noted his capacity for research. The author knew nothing of the lost research opportunities which the sensitive suggests, nor had he perceived or considered the latent research potentialities, evidently already observed by others, in the physician's character.

(3) The physician stated that at one time his family had owned very large tracts of land in a particular county in Ireland. Even in his own time lawsuits had proceeded in regard to the titles to these estates. His family had lost them. It was still almost dangerous for any of his family name to visit that county, so tense were the feelings that had been evoked in the past.

Both his mother and grandmother were only daughters, both had suffered from exophthalmic goitre, a complaint that suggested the stress under which they had lived which these circumstances had developed and accentuated. It gives an indirect indication of the heritage of nervous tension that had descended in some measure to the physician.

(4) Any person who has lived in Ireland knows of the persecutions and injustices which took place before the Catholic Emancipation Act was successfully passed through Parliament and of the residue of animosity which has remained.

The sensitive was not informed that the physician's family were Catholics but appears to have appreciated this fact at once, and its position and significance in the psychological picture she was drawing. None of these facts were known to the author or the sensitive prior to her investigation.

(5) The physician knew nothing of the incarceration of an ancestor next referred to. He stated that later he put the enquiry to a senior relative, who replied: " Sure, there wasn't one of your ancestors who wasn't in prison at some time."

(6) He was aware that there was a tradition in his family that one of their number had escaped from a fire, but he could not verify it. It is highly suggestive of the origin of his own experience of horror in the narrow built-in lane, with smoke and steam issuing from the bakery.

(7) With reference to his own early experiences:

An elder brother had informed him that he had been locked into a small room on a past occasion. This had not been for punishment, but owing to the fact that every member of the family had to go out he was locked into the room so that he should not get into mischief before their return. Darkness falling, the small boy would naturally be terrified. This thoughtless action on their part led to disastrous consequences.

(8) The last reference of the sensitive to an event that was not at the time quite clear to her obviously referred to the adventure of the large box or pen.

The physician stated that on reflection he remembered distinctly that when the box descended over him he tried his hardest, at the time, to recall another experience he had suffered of darkness and terror, but neither then or later had it ever come back into his conscious memory. This illustrates the depth of repression of recollections of experiences of horror in childhood.

Both of these experiences, however, were visualized clearly by the sensitive. As is usual with her reports, all irrelevant detail is sedulously suppressed. Only the salient incidents, which play their part in building up the complex, are preserved. They are all that are required in treatment, and the less detail there is the less is there to confuse and detract from the significance of the essentials when applied to the mind of the patient.

While this record was being discussed by the author and the physician he asked for advice. Should he endeavour to trace and confirm the facts recorded? He was advised that while from the scientific aspect it might be of value to pursue the matter further, from his own point of view he should clearly not do so. He should adopt the attitude that he had now fathomed, at last, all the causes that had led to his disturbing attacks of claustrophobia. That he should realize that they were of the past and finished with. He would never suffer again in consequence from them. He should therefore never dwell on them. He should supress them from his daily thoughts and allow them to lie forgotten in his subconscious mind for he had realized their lack of significance in his daily life.

He should dismiss them as quickly and completely as possible. On the other hand, he should dwell on the tribute to his unusual mental endowments, ingenuously expressed and come to him by accident, without his own seeking. As they concurred with the author's own unsought opinion, he should search diligently for wider scope for their expression. It would be to his own advantage and that of the community whose needs he served. This was the most important part of the record to him.

This last expression of opinion was emphasized, for this reason: where deeply rooted old-standing race-fear associations are being liquidated and their effect erased from an individual's consciousness, it is the height of folly to leave an absolute void in their place. The empty space could be refilled by the same complex, or another, particularly if the subject is dwelt upon. Give the mind something real and tangible to work upon, ambitions to realize, purposes to fulfil. Thus only can the complete eradication of the neurosis be ensured. This will undoubtedly be the case with this highly endowed young physician, whose future will be followed with the greatest interest.

CASES VII, VIII, IX. THREE CASES OF ASTHMA

A MEDICAL STUDENT, aged twenty-two years, consulted for persistent asthma. His case was investigated.

There was no family history of asthma whatsoever. He stated that the original attack of asthma had followed a catarrhal attack of an influenzal nature, six years previously.

He had been treated at that time by two courses of weekly injections of a stock anti-catarrhal prophylactic vaccine (not a stock anti-asthma vaccine); he stated that each injection (as might for this reason have been anticipated) produced a profound reaction, so severe that he was compelled to stay in bed, almost unable to inspire or expire for at least three days. In spite of his sufferings the treatment was persisted in, and he was told that the reactions were curative. He stated that he received twenty-four inoculations, and was manifestly worse at their termination. He had since taken adrenalin continuously and required about two cubic centimetres a day. He found that the attacks were worse at night, and also that they came on so severely before his examinations that he had to take adrenalin through the actual examination and his medical progress had been greatly retarded, and he had missed his examination and his year.

On investigation it was found that his arms were pitted with punctures. His breathing was much obstructed by asthmatic spasm. Very little catarrh appeared to be present in his lungs. Nevertheless, a vaccine was prepared from nasal and throat swabs, and administered in small doses for three months without any benefit. Meanwhile all feathers were removed from his bedroom, and attempts by various means to determine any particular protein that he might have become sensitive to were made without any success.

Next non-specific desensitization with a course of peptone injections led to very great improvement and he ceased attending for six months.

At this stage he brought his mother for consultation. She was a school-teacher, aged fifty-nine years; she was suffering from high blood-pressure, excessive weight and violent headaches. Treatment was prescribed. On the following day she became unconscious. She was treated in hospital and recovered consciousness in three days. On investigation she was considered to have suffered from acute cerebral oedema. Further less violent attacks occurred, and in spite of all treatment she slowly succumbed with progressive cerebral deterioration and died in four months.

At the period of his mother's first attack of unconsciousness the attacks of asthma recurred severely in the son; particularly at night. Peptone injections were recommended. They proved quite ineffective. The stage was reached when other measures had to be adopted. The

57

continuous palliative use of adrenalin, it was considered, would ultimately lead to serious consequences. The more violent spasms occurred at night, and the fact of their occurrence at a time of anxiety about his mother (his father was dead some years) both suggested that a nervous complex might be aggravating his condition. His psychological background was therefore investigated. His fountain-pen was utilized for the purpose. The following record was received :

" The owner of this pen, or the one who has handled it most, has much latent ability, and also a highly strung temperament. He suffers from a lack of conceit, of real belief in his own powers. His is extreme diffidence. These are minor factors in regard to his illness.

There is a strong bond between him and his mother. He is probably unconscious of its strength. But it has a considerable influence working through his subconscious mind upon his nervous system.

I see that when he was very young, probably only a baby, he had an illness in which he was gravely frightened. I think he has no memory of that illness, or of the fear it bequeathed to him. There was feverishness and it was connected with some difficulty in breathing. His mother was looking after him then, and was the all-important figure in his life.

All the baby's trust was in the mother. Trust seems betrayed to a small child when that all-powerful protector, the mother, fails to shelter the baby from terror. The small child has then an unreasoning feeling of desertion and helplessness. So it was in this case. The feeling of helplessness is illustrated in the patient's case by the failure of the mind to function and control the body at moments of strain when there is over-anxiety. This complex of temporary helplessness was created in the subconscious mind of the little child by the illness-terror connected with the difficulty in breathing. In later life it would therefore be likely to be associated with the apparatus for breathing.

This young man is conscientious. He is anxious as soon as possible to become qualified as a doctor and no longer be a burden to his mother. The recent treatment of his asthma was excellent and would have cured the average patient completely.

The fact that this man gets a return of the trouble seems largely due to this complex I have mentioned. It lay dormant in his unconscious mind and would have remained so if it had not been roused to life by some very mistaken treatment, an overdose of something, given him when he first had asthma, which made him seriously ill, and having that immense difficulty with his breathing. It was—though from a different cause—analogous to that brief but terrifying condition when he was a baby, which I have just described.

The old unreasoning infantile terror is now active, and the cause of these nervous spasms. The terror received a double vitality from the shock of the mother's sudden illness. The mother's brief unconsciousness produced anticipation of her death. The mother remains the one protector in the man's subconscious mind. Her sudden serious illness helped to produce the old situation in his subconscious mind—the baby's feeling of helplessness and desertion by his guardian. And though the mother recovered temporarily the harm was done—the old infantile terror given artificial life. The young man should be made to realize that his asthma is now purely artificial.

It should have no reality in his present life, for it comes out of the dead past. The past is finished, done with. He must realize that these nervous spasms are produced by a purely irrational terror. And knowing now what it is, from henceforth he will have no difficulty in breathing. The physical cause of his illness has been removed by the recent treatment. So he will have no return of the nervous asthmatic spasms. He has no cause for fear of his examinations. He will be entirely free from asthma when he faces his examiners, once he has definitely grasped and accepted the fundamental cause of the asthmatic condition.

The root cause was infantile terror associated with breathing in childhood. Failure of the protecting mother to shield him from that terror.

In adult life again difficulty in breathing from a genuine attack of asthma. Repetition of childish experience through failure of a doctor who gave him an overdose of the wrong remedy, so that he was reduced to a state of helpless misery by the adult's protector.

Sudden illness of mother, anticipation of her death, roused the old feeling of desertion by the fundamental protector.

Minor factors springing from complex-diffidence, lack of belief in his own first-rate ability.''

This report was read and explained to the patient. The psychological factor associated with his ailment was emphasized. The prospect of complete recovery was indicated, together with a successful future. In spite of the fact that his mother's illness was rapidly progressing towards an inevitable fatal issue, the patient's asthmatic attacks subsided at once. The peptone injections were at once discontinued. Only once has he used adrenalin since, on the night after his mother died. Some weeks later he suffered from an attack of epidemic influenza and spent a week in bed. Though catarrh accompanied the illness, no asthmatic attacks recurred. The patient appears to be completely cured of his disability.

In considering the progress of this case the following points emerge:

(1) As every immunologist knows, asthmatics are exceedingly sensitive to bacterial proteins. The greatest care is necessary in the process of desensitizing them. It is better far to err on the safe side and administer too small, rather than too large a dose. Too large a dose, besides producing a severe spasm, tends to make the patient still more sensitive and more difficult to desensitize, as occurred in this case, when enormous overdoses were given.

(2) The importance of the psychological factor in maintaining or initiating asthma is suggested. And the possibility of removing a buried complex by disclosing it.

(3) A catarrh initiated the first attack in his case. Probably the non-specific desensitizing with peptone relieved it.

(4) The second attack was undoubtedly purely psychological, initiated by anxiety about his mother. By unravelling the underlying complex recovery from the asthmatic attacks appears to be permanent.

I should like to add and emphasize that with reference to any medical case of this type dealt with in this manner it is essential that every possible physical cause of the syndrome of symptoms observed should be eliminated before any attempt to deal with a suppositious psychological basis is made. This is partly for the reason that if an individual is suffering from chronic sepsis, secondary anæmia, debility, etc., it is far more difficult to remove a psychological injury than if the individual's physical condition is at its best. Moreover, the removal of the sepsis, anæmia, catarrh, or whatever it may be, may of itself be sufficient to relieve the psychological aspect, manifest or suspect.

Such a course was adopted in this case; only after the failure of physical measures were psychological means employed. Since writing these notes the later history of the case is submitted. It is as follows:

He passed his first examination, his previous stumbling-block, without difficulty five months later.

A year later he consulted again in great anxiety. He stated the asthma had returned suddenly at night. Careful examination revealed no evidence of asthma, and he was told so most emphatically. It transpired that in ten days the next examination was due.

He was given five cubic centimetres of his own blood, freshly drawn, by injections into his buttocks—it was at the same time re-emphasized that he had no asthma.

He returned the next day and stated that either the lecture he had received or the injection had cured him.

He was given a further injection, and in a few days passed his examination without difficulty.

A year later he passed the final examination for his medical degree without experiencing any nervous difficulties, and went immediately to England to join the R.A.M.C. Served in Malay and smuggled a Japanese sword home, which he presented to the writer. He is now in practice in England.

CASE VIII

Miss L., aged nineteen years. Consulted for asthma. She gave the history that she had suffered from asthma in increasing intensity for four years.

During part of this period she had worked in London for a year as an assistant to a dentist. The asthma had become worse and she started using adrenalin, which had benefited her for a time. The condition became so crippling that she was forced to return, but found that she could not now live in her old home, which on careful enquiry appeared to be a healthy, well situated farmhouse. She lived with an aunt in a neighbouring town. So far as she knew, none of her family suffered from asthma.

On examination she was found to be suffering from severe asthma, without any marked catarrh but considerable chest deformity from constant spasm. She was treated for four months with an autogenous vaccine, various antispasmodic drugs, a course of stilboestrol, and her general health was attended to and improved.

Very slight, if any, benefit to the asthma resulted. Owing to the physician living at a distance from her home it was found impossible to continue treatment. A course of peptone desensitization was started, which she carried out herself under direction, and she wrote stating that she had improved considerably.

A year later she reported in person that the asthma had relapsed and was as bad as when she started treatment. She was given an asthma exercise pamphlet with directions. She was tested against various proteins (Bencard) and was found to be slightly sensitive to cereals, vegetables and fruits.

It was impossible to pursue this line of research and treatment.

A specimen of her handwriting was obtained and examined.

The following record was obtained:

" This is the handwriting of a sensitive woman with great natural ability. But she suffers from extreme diffidence, and there is conflict in her unconscious mind. She was working for a time in a large city, and the conditions there had a psychological effect, helping to induce the nervous asthmatic condition. It enhanced her feeling of diffidence, being among a strange people, and also one minute individual among millions of different human beings. It was a subconscious rather than a conscious feeling which found an outlet in her consciousness in nervous asthma. Now why was the consciousness affected to such a degree? It is because there is a complex in her unconscious mind, created by racial memory, and by an early experience.

When she was a tiny child she happened to be alone towards dusk one evening. The people in her home were preoccupied by some bad news. The sensitive child sensed that they were disturbed and alarmed. They told her not to go out of the house and to keep quiet. Their alarm had made her uneasy, and a little frightened, too. Then, hurt by their preoccupation (for she had been petted and was usually a centre of attraction), she wandered out of the house into the grey twilight. A strong wind was blowing. She went into a field in which cattle were grazing. She felt unhappy and uneasy. When some way down the field, she remembered that she had been told not to go out of the house again. Feeling guilty, she turned to go home. A young bullock came towards her. To the child it seemed enormous. It lowered its head, coming right up to her. Terrified, she turned and ran up the hill against the wind. Soon she was gasping for breath, her little legs barely carrying her. Then her feet tripped in the root of a tree and she tumbled forward into a hollow, and was winded. She lay gasping for breath in this hollow, or pit, in an agony of terror. She expected the big monster that had followed her would trample on her and destroy her. When at last breath came regularly again she saw the bullock standing at the edge of the pit watching her. It was waiting, she felt, to destroy her if she got up and tried to go home.

In that big field, in the grey twilight, she was utterly alone in what she imagined was terrible danger, and for the first time in her life she was deserted by the providence of the small child, the protecting grown-up people. Paralysed with fear, she screamed and screamed. No one came. It grew darker and wilder in the big field. She seemed to be there an age before the bullock eventually moved off. Somehow she crawled out of the pit and ran for home. But again she lost her breath, and again what was only a playful young bullock followed her. When she did reach the house she in time recovered her breath. But she was scolded for disobedience, and for the mud on her clothes. Coupled then with the experience of fear was the feeling of guilt, and these were associated with loss of breath, with incapacity to breathe. The experience made a terrible impression on the little child's mind. She didn't relieve it by telling of it to anyone because it was associated with disobedience. So intolerable was the experience that the consciousness of the small girl did what happens customarily in the case of a bad fear experience with small children; it buried in the subconscious mind the haunting memory of what was to her a ghastly time of unearthly terror. In other words while the subconscious retained it her conscious mind suppressed it. So it became a complex.

The complex became active when she was grown up and produced this nervous asthma. She lived for a time working in the big city.

There she had that feeling of minuteness among millions of people, and with it came the accompanying feeling of loneliness associated with the big field. Then in her subconsciousness the huge city gradually grew into the huge monster—the bullock—that had terrified her so long ago. So the nervous asthma again became the expression

E

of that experience when she had been winded and was choking for breath.

The race memory went back a long way. Some of her ancestors were oppressed. One of them was a rebel and fought with poor weapons against the monstrous might of disciplined soldiers. He was taken prisoner and hanged in the presence of his wife, who was carrying a child. She imparted to the child in her womb the awful terror and distress occasioned by the sight of her husband choking for breath, dying on the gallows. That child developed nervous asthma in later life. It helped to produce in the physical body the tendency to asthma among certain of the descendants of this woman. Some of them of course, did not take after her. But a majority had the tendency, which if the life and experience were healthy, did not lead them to develop asthma.

The patient should be told that this early experience of hers is the cause of the attacks, this cause being assisted and accentuated by the racial memory. Tell her that it belongs to the past, that it is something therefore dead and done with. Knowing this, she is not going any longer to lose her breath and be seized by these bad attacks that spring from the fateful hour when she was terrified and winded.''

This account was read to her and psychological treatment based on this explanation was instituted and was reinforced by occasional correspondence. Nine months later she wrote that she considered she was cured.

A year later she called to ask for a certificate of health; she was free from asthma, and she wished to cross to England to join the British Army.

On careful examination, a certificate was found justified; her health appeared perfect.

In this case there is no doubt that the psychological cause of the patient's asthma was the preponderating one.

It is interesting to note that at one period she could not live in her old home, where presumably the supposed complex was established. It had not been possible to verify this.

The ancestral experience appears to have been largely secondary in this case—merely rendering her nervous system sensitive. The primary factor was without doubt the repressed experience in connection with the young bullock.

CASE IX. THE CASE OF MRS. T.

WHILE a considerable number of patients who have suffered from asthma, have been completely cured, by desensitization and various other physical methods, there remains a group that may be classed as recurrent, who from time to time, light up with attacks of more or less severe asthmatic states, which again subside under treatment for six months, or so, or even for years, and then flare up again.

In such cases it is an inevitable conclusion that the nervous system of the individual is predisposed. As an illustration of this point, the writer of these notes has observed two patients over a matter of fifteen years. Both have suffered from chronic nasal infection during the whole period. The patient with the more severe infection has never suffered from asthma. The second patient whose case is under review, has suffered from intermittent but severe asthmatic attacks with only slight catarrh during the whole period. She has been desensitised a number of times, with bacterial vaccine, peptone injections, house dust preparations, etc. These treatments have been of great benefit from time to time, sometimes several years, but if anxiety, over-work, strain, supervene, the asthmatic condition tends to recur, and recent attacks, though not so violent as earlier ones, became a periodic disability and led the writer to investigate her psychological background by ESP.

Though it was not expected that recovery would occur, the psychological treatment, it was hoped, would reinforce other measures and be of value in her general treatment.

The patient, a lady of forty-eight years, started mild attacks of asthma at the age of five years.

At twenty-six with her first pregnancy and confinement she had very severe asthma.

She had two daughters, the eldest suffered mildly, the second severely, from asthma as both grew up. Recurrent less severe attacks occurred twice or thrice yearly with the mother. An important point relevant to these notes is the probable hereditary factor.

The lady was of a strikingly vivacious temperament with considerable social capacities, and the writer had always supposed a French Hugenot strain. When the following investigation had been made, the lady herself admitted that the Spanish history to be recorded, was an established family tradition. This ESP investigation is now submitted.

SENSITIVE'S REPORT

" The writer of this note is an extremely interesting character. She is capable, vivacious and has great charm. Her social gifts may be traced back to a group of aristocratic ancestors in the far past. But there is also in the racial memories of pronounced insecurity, fear, due to experiences of ancestors. The influence of this fear, which comes from the unconscious mind, makes her unduly anxious at times about little things and are a contributory cause of the asthma. The racial history and a certain experience of hers when she was very young to a great extent produce the conditions of breathlessness. I will begin the racial history.

I get a southern country—a Spanish nobleman. He belonged to one of the leading families of Spain and had a daughter Isabella. She fell in love with a man who was her father's steward and not of her class. Juan, the steward, and she eloped. They were secretly married by a priest. To a Spanish grandee like her father this marriage for his daughter was the uttermost degradation. He would rather have seen her dead than married to one beneath her in station. His son sought out Juan and in an affray wounded him gravely. He was ill for a long time as a result of the injury received. All the money was spent during his illness. The young couple became very poor. When Isabella was carrying a child she, who had been used to spacious rooms, lived in a filthy little den in a street full of smells. One hot airless summer's day when she felt she would die of suffocation, she gave birth to this child. This experience and her further tragic experiences in a life of hunger and unspeakable squalor left a deep impression on the racial memory; for the sufferer was a delicately nurtured woman with a strong passionate temperament. Her father, when appealed to, would only forgive her if she gave up her husband and returned home. She would not do this, and her husband being a weak character, just drifted, idling, never making good. So she died of poverty and semi starvation. The son became a sailor and was in a shipwreck off the coast of Scotland. I do not know when; but he married and settled in that country. He was very like his mother and always carried with him the memory of her sufferings, and he had also inherited her vivacity and charm.

Later in the history of the family Mary's ancestors, who were Scottish landowners of good birth, backed the wrong side in a war, I think, connected with the Stuarts. One of them spent many years in an evil smelling airless dungeon in which he was imprisoned by the victors of the war. He was at times nearly asphyxiated in it. So the old Spanish memory was renewed, strengthened, and the nervous habit of breathlessness induced. Thus the Spanish ancestress and this descendant suffered agony from the real terror of suffocation. It is the strong emotional memory that abides in the unconscious race mind. He eventually escaped from prison, but the child of his marriage then was deeply impressed by his father's sub-conscious memories of that time, and in consequence suffered from asthma. For a long time the family was very poor. First there was the fugitive hunted life of the father, then the insecurity fear of the descendants who could not get enough to eat owing to their poverty. Though a few generations later they knew better days the racial memory of the airless dungeon, of insecurity and danger became ineffaceable, and in a disguised form was expressed in attacks of breathlessness.

There was one minor factor in the experience of an ancestor married to a sea captain. She went with him on one of his voyages. The ship met with storms. She was very ill in an airless berth, and her fears that she would die while lying in this bunk in a tiny cabin all deeply impressed her direct descendants' unconscious mind, and the other racial memories in it, that might have faded with time, obtained new life.

When the present descendant, Mary, was little more than a baby, a woman who was a maid in charge of her, punished her for naughtiness by shutting her up in a cubby hole of a room for an hour or two. The child became terrified as her mind linked up with the unconscious racial memories — again the airless dungeon, the filthy den in Spain and again the insecurity feeling of ancestors. She was gasping for breath when she was let out by the nurse and very cold. She was ill then—a bronchial attack from the chill caught and was very breathless and feverish. A child instinctively represses from her conscious memory any experience of great fear. So Mary is not likely to recollect this terrifying episode. Also as a very small child she was taken to the sea one day and was made to go into the water which frightened her, some ill-advised elder ducked her. She choked and had an attack of breathlessness that was a painful and alarming experience.

All these racial and personal experiences produced a formidable complex that lay in the subconscious mind and expresses itself in attacks of asthma. But Mary must say to herself that these fear experiences belong to the dead past and therefore are finished with, over, and cannot any longer affect her by producing breathlessness as they did numbers of her ancestors. If she truly realises this cause of her asthma—that it is due to a great extent to the emotional fear reactions in a past that is over, her asthma attacks will gradually lessen and finally cease altogether.

But there is one contributory factor to them. She appears to live in what I might call an asthmatic house. It is low lying and somewhat shut in, people who lived there before her time were asthmatic. If Mary had not a tendency through inherited fear to asthma she would not be affected by this house. But definitely it is harmful, not a good place to live in for anyone who has the tendency to get breathless.

It is possible that certain physical exercises for asthma would be useful. They would certainly be useful in the case of her daughters. But the root cause of her type of illness lies in the complex created by a series of past terrible ancestral experiences, most of them racial, and the effect of these can be banished by a realisation of their present unreality.

She has a clever brain and the sensitive imagination that is definitely Celtic, that comes from her Celtic ancestors. Though this imagination is a great asset in life it makes her more sensitive to worries, and coupled with the racial fear it leads her to stiffen up physically and helps to bring on asthma. When this worrying and feeling of tension possesses her, it would be well for her to go and sit in an easy chair or lie in a half reclining position and endeavour to relax every muscle in her body and at the same time relax her mind deliberately directing it into the channel of pleasant thoughts of happy moments in her life in a dreamy way. In other words, she should seek *stillness* for a while through the relaxation of her whole being. This means acquiring a new habit of mind and may be difficult at first, but it will serve her well if she practises it in the right way, and it will improve her health.''

Since this ancestral and family background has been submitted to the patient and she has had psychological treatment based on its findings she has enjoyed a period of comparatively complete freedom from asthma. There is no question it has been of great help in her treatment; moreover she has been subject to severe strain during the period since her last attack. This last attack, in the writer's opinion, was brought about by anxiety attendant on her eldest daughter's marriage.

After her recovery, both her mother-in-law, and her father, died in her house. Both, though old, died with some abruptness. These experiences provided conditions of anxiety and shock for the patient. No asthma recurred —nor after the recent marriage of her second daughter.

With reference to the report, it may also be mentioned that the house is as described.

It was previously occupied by a large family, amongst whom were several asthmatics. They were known of by the writer but not by the patient or sensitive.

One cannot fail to note the fact that the patient suffered from severe ashma during her first pregnancy. The writer was not aware of this until after the report was written. It will be recalled that the confinement of the suppositious Spanish ancestress occurred in airless suffocating conditions, enough to form the foundation point of a complex. In addition, there is the statement that a Spaniard, an ancestor, had been in a shipwreck off the coast of Scotland and later had married in this country. There was a family tradition to this effect. Members of the patient's family often told her that she must have taken after the Spanish ancestor. She had only one sister, who is of a slower, more phlegmatic disposition and has never suffered from asthma. Four further years have passed and she is still free from asthma.

CASE X. A CASE OF AMNESIA

THE lack of adequate explanation of the factors involved in the following case, the very obscurity of its psychological background, whether such a background did exist and could be used with any effect in the very serious position in which the patient found himself, led to the employment of ESP in its investigation. Briefly the history was as follows :

The young man involved, aged twenty-five years, had had a normal, uneventful life. He came of vigorous stock, had a sheltered healthy childhood, passed through his school years happily and without difficulty, entered his father's business, appeared to establish himself quickly and successfully. He seemed to his medical attendant who had observed him during the whole period to be a young man of energy, strength and purpose, sincerity, capacity and of distinct promise. If anything, he may have expressed slight over-confidence in his own undoubted ability.

He married eminently, suitably and happily. He had one child. Unfortunately at birth damage had been done to its brachial plexus, and although the most expert surgical help had been obtained one arm had remained weak and somewhat undeveloped.

At this stage his medical attendant was engaged to attend a further confinement; he had not been employed in the first. At about the eighth month the patient's brother called and gave the startling information that the patient had disappeared. It was explained that on occasions recently he had suffered from alcoholism; that he had lost control of himself more than once, and that his father contemplated dismissing him from the business. From his history, his upbringing, his character and his temperament, the story appeared utterly fantastic. It proved to be correct.

He was traced. He was suffering from acute alcoholism. His immediate physical symptoms were controlled without difficulty. The question that became insistent in the family physician's mind was :

How could immediate disaster to his career be prevented? And how could disaster be prevented from

74

occurring from a probable recurrence of alcoholism at a later date ?

It was necessary to interview his parents, his wife's parents and his wife. Their co-operation was essential. They were asked to renew their sorely shaken confidence in him. Absolute confidence on their part, rather than threats of dismissal, was essential to his recovery.

It was inferred that shock at the injury to his daughter's arm and the imminence of a further confinement were factors of great importance in his recent lapse. When questioned about his recent attack he stated frankly that a blank came over his mind, that he was not conscious of doing anything until he suddenly found himself suffering from alcoholic poisoning and utterly ashamed of his condition. He stated that it had occurred in that manner previously.

He was reassured about his recovery. That the lapse was almost certainly due to some cause for which he was not responsible, that it could be investigated further, that he need have no anxiety about his wife or for his future.

The investigation made from his handwriting was as follows :

"August 5th, 1936.

I feel that this man is highly sensitive in certain respects. He has plenty of latent ability. But there is for him an obstacle in his deeper mind that at times seems to prey upon him, that he tries to escape from into unconsciousness. I mean that the directive part of his mind seeks release, or rather endeavours to evade this thing, by taking either drink or drugs.

I get a sense of persecution. But this feeling of persecution is old and comes from the race-memory. Some ancestor of his underwent persecution in some form

75

which I will get at later. However, the patient when very young — scarcely more than a baby — was terrified by some, to him, large animal, and this terror left a vivid impression on his mind. It helped to link him up with the older race terror, and in fact to break down the ordinary defences the subconscious mind has evolved which prevent the flow of the race-memory from penetrating into the consciousness.

It seems as if some long way back his people were hunted and fugitives. I feel that they were persecuted and I get the sense of continual insecurity in consequence. It is not like a sudden and agonizing period of torture, but of a long chronic fear oppressing these people. Some of his ancestors were Irish and during this period never had security of tenure in their home. The wars led to their being plundered, harassed and slaughtered. At an earlier time than this era of war this man's people were Catholics. I see the reign of Elizabeth and a place some distance from here. One of his race was tortured for belonging to the Catholic faith by the people of the Reformed Church. I see that he was burnt and that his wife and children had to hide from the persecutors, escaping to a hilly country. Their name was not P— then. These come from the female side, I think. One of the children married into the P—family. That seems clear.

Later on I get the sense that they settled down and knew prosperous times. But it seems that there was a personal tragedy, perhaps a hundred years ago, which left a marked impression on the race-memory.

One of the family seems to have been a soldier, and came home to his wife with serious wounds, at the time when she was going to have a baby. The sudden appearance of her husband, broken and dying, carried

76

into her presence, terrified her and built up, or rather renewed, the old terror. This may have occurred about a hundred years ago. It is hard to read the time. However, the patient had one outbreak not far from the time his wife was going to have, or had just had, a baby. I am not quite sure whether it was before or after the event. But the inherited fear that remained from this personal tragedy of the ancestor was roused by subconscious anxiety about his wife and led to a loss of memory in which the fear dominated, clouding everything, also making him drink. There is no evil in this man. He is simply the victim of a repressed fear.

But none of the old memories could affect the patient if it were not for the shock he received as a baby. I would suggest to him that he is not going to have any return of the desire to break out as he did. For the cause of it is now removed.

You have treated him wisely and I want you to keep on impressing his people that they must give him every chance to make good. There is no real badness in the patient. What he needs is encouragement and the assurance of those near to him that they believe he will make good; that the past is over and done with; that they trust him in the future and know that he will not let them down. He will not remember, nor will anyone else probably, that early terror he experienced which was the principal cause operating. For it is from this terror plus the racial fear he tried to escape. But knowing them now he is finished with them, and they no longer have any influence over his life. Yes, your treatment is excellent . . . . . It is merely a race fear by which at certain times his subconscious mind is oppressed. Knowing this he is not going to yield again to the desire for escape by taking any stimulant that clouds his memory and brain.

Let him realize that he has work of a kind that is important because his success in it will bring happines to his people; that he is responsible for their happiness, so is not going to surrender to the fantasy of fear conjured up by the primitive section of his mind. It is a bogey which has no existence in reality. Insist on this idea. He should, too, so far as is possible, lead a healthy life out of doors when he is not working. If he can tire his body with healthy exertions his mind will be more likely to remain perfectly normal.

Use your own discretion as to what you tell him in regard to what I have written.

The great thing is to give him plenty of occupation that interests him apart from work, and assure him that he has considerable ability and that it is up to him to develop it and so make a success of his life. He will do well if he bears this in mind.

At night before he sleeps let him suggest to himself that on the next day he is going absolutely straight, will do his work well, and then enjoy his recreations. You can put all this into simple words for him. But as I see it your treatment could not be improved so far. Continue on the same lines."

This report proved of the greatest help in the treatment of this case. It was read to the patient. It was pointed out that the cause of his lapse was in the past and that he was not to blame for it. That its effect was over. This in a great measure restored his confidence in himself. His wife gave birth to a healthy son a month after his illness, with no unfortunate birth accident to mar the event, as had been feared.

He has had no further trouble.

The Sensitive's report in this case, while no proof can be adduced to establish the correctness or otherwise of the explanation built up of the cause of the psycho-neurosis, nevertheless is of significance, in that it draws attention to the probable considerable importance of the race heritage in such cases. It is illustrated in the linking-up of the race heritage with the immediate tragedy in the patient's own life, the birth injury to his first child when the psycho-neurosis first manifested itself.

Much, no doubt, depends on the manner in which such a report is utilized. Its judicious employment appeared to have been instrumental in restoring self-confidence and to have been a factor of importance in re-establishing continuous conscious control in the mind of the patient.

It may be mentioned that the Sensitive was neither informed of the nature of the treatment that had been employed before she was consulted nor of that part of the treatment that had been directed to impressing the patient's family. (Twenty years have elapsed. There has been no relapse.)

CASE XI.   A NEUROSIS OF " CHOKING "
(Cured by J. Murphy, M.D., with the assistance of the same sensitive.)

I HAD to attend a lady with a chronic complaint which confined her to her bed for a considerable time and caused some anxiety.

Her husband consulted me during this time for a feeling of smothering of a troublesome type, together with other peculiar symptoms about which a written statement was obtained from him which is submitted.

His wife stated that frequently in the night her husband disturbed her by rushing into her room grunting as if he

79

were choking. He invariably opened the window and took several gasps of air, said he was better, and returned to bed. This disturbed her greatly, and naturally it was vital both for his wife and himself that the condition should be relieved.

His statement of his symptoms was as follows:

" I am just seventy years of age and a retired bank manager for two years.

In dry weather I wake up at night with a stuffiness of the nose and have to get up and walk about the house at all hours. I used to smoke about twenty cigarettes a day. Doctor says there is nothing wrong with my nose, heart or lungs; but he gave me a good prescription for a spray which gives me a certain relief.

I feel the complaint coming on if I even think of anything like the smell of creosote, and if my hands are dusty I have to dip them in water, as it appears to affect the stuffiness.

When the complaint appears I have to loosen the band of my trousers, as I feel all tightened up and stuffy, and at night no matter how cold the weather is I must have windows and even doors open, and if the windows were open (and I got it into my head at night) I must get up to confirm it. I have had the complaint in a much milder form for the last thirty-five years. I attributed it then to the dust on the roads, as I rode a motor-bicycle, and after a ride on a summer's day I had to dip my hands in cold water and sponge my face, not for the cause of cleanness, but to keep off the complaint. I am not a bit nervous about myself, but I fear the terrible feeling when it comes on. I feel I am smothering if I sleep in a small room, and I wake up with the feeling that I am being held down under a musty feather bed or mattress.

I could not dip my face into a basin of water at any
time even when a young chap, afraid of smothering, or
sniff up cold water out of my hand which a friend advised
me to do every morning. When the complaint comes on
at night I must have a light in the room or I would get
the smothering feeling if left in the dark."

He was evidently suffering from some unexplained
psycho-neurosis which caused a sensation of choking. It
was initiated in his youth, for he could recall it for at least
thirty-five years, and it had become worse lately.

It was decided to endeavour to discover the cause by
utilizing ESP, and the statement of his complaint was sent
to the sensitive.

The following reply was received from her:

" This man is interesting, for his complaint is not
primarily caused by any physical or mental defect. In
his case other people are the offenders, and he is the victim
of what took place in the far past. Though occasionally
a prey to fits of depression or over-anxiety, he is in no way
neurasthenic, and is a man of sound judgment whose advice
may be relied on in the affairs of life.

There are two factors at work in his case. One great
terror he experienced when so young that conscious memory
had scarcely begun to register events, and the subconscious
mind, which is deeply emotional, alone recorded them, and
therefore left a strong impression on his fundamental nature.
The second factor lies in his racial history.

I will first tell of the shock he experienced when a tiny
child. His mother, or the one most intimately associated
with him, who represented the mother to the baby, became
seriously ill; some other member of the household was also
ill.

It seems that the mother or nurse, the one whom the
baby regarded as his natural protector, was suddenly taken

from him. A strange young girl took her place. It was during hot weather in the summer. The girl took him out for an airing on a dusty road. There was a gusty wind which at intervals blew up clouds of dust. This would have made no impression if it had not been for what followed.

The child had been moved temporarily into a small stuffy room. The wind went down and there was a regular heat-wave. In the evening the girl put the child into his bath, then left him for a few moments there. He was too young to be left even for a moment in shallow water. Alone in that small room he became terrified, tried to struggle out of the tub, and in so doing rolled over so that his face was under water. This led to an acute spasm of terror in which he choked and swallowed water. The strange small room, the imprisonment in the bath, gave him the sense of being shut in in after-life, and led to the vehement desire to open windows and doors. This desire was also accentuated by his having to sleep in that airless room after this experience, and by the desertion of his natural protector, the sick woman.

When the girl came back the child was half suffocated from the water, and his struggle to breathe because of his terror at being in this position. She took him out of the bath quickly and roughly and when his breath came back he screamed. She struck him then to frighten him into being quiet. This act accentuated his fear. It made him wild with terror again, reproducing the idea of suffocation. Previous to the bath the girl had put him in clothes that were too tightly fastened round his little body, and during that day in the heat the acute discomfort of it had made him cry and led the strange girl, so unlike his natural protector, to be cross and impatient with him. The constriction of the baby's clothes remained therefore in his subconscious memory, and leads the elderly man to loosen his clothes when the complaint begins. He experiences again, then, those hours of a hot day when he was clad in too-tight garments and was looked after by an alarming stranger. The important point to remember is that this terror (lost to memory) would have made no impression of any consequence on the adult if it had not been for the desertion of the mother at that time; the mother represents, particularly to a highly bred sensitive child, his Providence, all-loving, all-powerful, who protects him in his defenceless condition.

The smell of creosote in conjunction with this illness is easily explained. It is analogous to a strong antiseptic smell which was used in that house of sickness. When taken to see his mother, the sick woman, the smell was strongly in her room. He was only with her for a moment or two and she was very feeble and white, and greatly changed in appearance. So he was again much frightened, and the fright became associated with that antiseptic smell pervading the room, and afterwards associated with the smell of creosote.

The boy was so young he forgot these incidents in his early life. In fact they were so associated with terror and shock that his unconscious mind made his consciousness forget them because of their unpleasant associations. But now the elderly man must face them and realize that the subconscious memory of that terror is the fundamental cause of that feeling of stuffiness, of being smothered. When he gets that terrible feeling he must realize he is merely living again that time of terror when he was helpless and defenceless in infancy. He should say to himself, ' The cause of my illness is no longer there, it is past, done with. I am no longer going to be the victim of a child's fantasy of terror, I am breathing freely and with ease. Knowing now the fear and shock that caused it, I shall no longer be a prey to it, to what is dead and done with—because it belongs to the past.'

This man should seek plenty of occupations, particularly of an out-of-door character, for when his attention is wholly caught and his consciousness interested there is much less chance of the subconscious thrusting on him the old terror which produces the complaint. The complaint was in a milder form when he was younger—partly because he led a busier and more occupied life and partly because early memories are more liable to haunt in age, particularly when there is also an influence from the racial memory involved, as in this case. This man had an ancestor, whom he resembled in temperament, who was in a shipwreck of some kind. At any rate he was for hours struggling in the water for his life and half suffocated and smothered by huge waves. There were other harrowing circumstances connected with this incident, too long to relate here. Though the ancestor lived a long time ago he had a temperament akin to that of the living descendant, and so the descendant at times tunes into this part of the racial memory, or rather his unconscious mind does so, and thereby induces, or accentuates, the terror-inspired tendency to gasp for breath. It gives to the sensation of being smothered and enclosed a greater vigour. This cause can be removed by being understood and thereby resolved.

The patient comes of a race of people that are in the majority aristocratic in the true sense of the word. That is to say, whatever their position, they were for generations gifted with a fine sensitiveness which led them to be almost morbidly honest about money and considerate for others. But such sensitivity leads the patient to be more open to a complaint of this type.

The doctor must insist that he is not in any way neurasthenic. He has merely been the victim of circumstances outside his control. Knowing them now, and using his common sense to resolve them, he can cure himself in time completely of his complaint.

Note for the physician, not to be shown to the patient:

This is an extremely difficult case owing to the age of the patient and the many years he has been subject to this malady in its milder form. It has a strong grip of him owing to its chronic character. So the revelation of the source of the complaint may not make a complete cure, though it should certainly improve matters. The early terror gave the patient also a lack of confidence in himself which may not be superficially apparent, but is there.

It lies with his physician, so far as he is able to build up confidence in the patient's mind and faith in his own power to cure himself by his making to the patient encouraging and positive suggestions."

As a result of a judicious use of this report the patient is already cured, and, despite his age, now fully believes that his illness is the direct inheritance of some shock he got in his very early youth. He disclosed a very interesting story which runs parallel with the report. He explained that fifty or sixty years ago there were women at every sea-side resort in Ireland known as " dippers." Their function was to dip small children in the sea, for which criminal act they received a few coppers from the parent. He remembers being at Bray for the summer, and being handed over to a forbidding-looking corpulent " dipper," until he was absolutely terrified of his life. One day his mother had to go to town shopping and she decided to give him to the dipper for a few hours. He became scared and decided to escape at the first opportunity. When such a chance was presented to him he absconded, but was followed by the dipper and caught. As a punishment she not only dipped him in the sea several times but held him under for what he thought was an eternity.

He felt a sense of choking and was scared almost to death. He remembers shaking all over with fright, and this made a terrible and lasting impression on his subconscious mind. He blames this for the attacks, but doesn't at all deny the probability of the bath incident mentioned in the report, as he was too young to remember it.

Some six years have passed. The patient has recently again affirmed his complete recovery.

CASE XII. THE DEAD HANDS
ILLUSTRATING HOW TRAUMA CAN UNCOVER A PSYCHO-NEUROSIS
(Written during the Second World War.)

OUR judgment of the actions of others is sometimes formed with perhaps too little reflection on the causes from which they spring. We are perhaps too ready to ascribe blame. Do we make a comprehensive assessment of all the tendencies and motives that lead to the actions which we are judging? Do we consider fully the factors that influence us in the various actions that we take and the decisions we have to make? These reflections and questions arise and confront the investigator when considering the following case.

The patient was a Jew, a young man of twenty-seven years. He came for consultation about a year ago. His history, showed that he had been eminently successful before the war in the business he had taken up. He had been advanced over several senior employees and had been made manager of an important branch of his firm. Owing to failure of supplies from war conditions the firm was driven to close all its branches. He had to seek other employment. *He accepted* the post of a fireman in a city in Northern Ireland, in default of any more suitable employment.

A week prior to consultation, during an official inspection, and while saluting, he brought his hand down sharply and struck the fire-pump, which was standing close behind him. At this point in his account he broke down surprisingly. He stated he had obtained an X-ray at once. He had not been able to sleep since. He was afraid for his hand. It was a terrible thing—his hands! He thought he had better return home; could anything be done?

Examination of the injured hand showed moderate swelling and a small traumatic ganglion on the extensor tendon sheath of the little finger. Nothing more. There was no metacarpal or phalangeal fracture. This was clearly evident without recourse to any X-ray. Nor did the manner by which the injury was incurred suggest sufficient force to produce fracture.

The exaggerated psychological effect of a comparatively trivial injury appeared to be out of all proportion. It wanted something more than mere ordinary pain or hypersensitiveness to account for the fear. He appeared to suffer from acute psychological shock and nausea.

He had unusually long artistic hands with firm delicate fingers. On enquiry he admitted to being an expert amateur pianist. He was undoubtedly of a highly strung sensitive nature. But there seemed to be something more. He had not slept, he stated, for a week, and he had travelled a distance of 260 miles to his home over what appeared to be physically a trivial accident.

Everything possible was done to reassure him. He was told repeatedly that complete recovery was certain.

As elaborate treatment as possible was prescribed. Still he seemed doubtful and quite surprisingly unsatisfied and unconvinced by the opinion given.

In an endeavour to re-establish his confidence the principles of psychological inheritance were explained to him. It was suggested to him that some misfortune associated with the hands had in all probability occurred to some ancestor of his; that he was allowing himself to be influenced unduly by the subconscious memories which he had inherited. This was quite unnecessary, he should not be influenced. This also failed to relieve his anxiety.

Finally it was suggested to him that this factor could be investigated further by ESP, which also was explained to him. As this suggestion seemed to relieve his mind unexpectedly, his fountain-pen was borrowed and submitted to a sensitive. The sensitive was informed of the nature and circumstances of the injury, and of the possibility of underlying psychological factors complicating the case. The following record was obtained by her:

"The owner of this pen is an interesting person, for he has a high degree of intelligence and a remarkably good brain. Physically he is perfectly normal. But it is his misfortune and handicap that some distance back in his racial history terrible and brutal cruelty left a deep mark or brand on the subconscious mind of his race. There is a subconscious as well as physical heredity. Not merely the physical attributes but the subconscious attributes can be passed on from generation to generation. The cruelty I have mentioned led to the development of an over-sensitive nervous system. In fortunate and peaceful circumstances, or when nothing in the life-events of people of this family are in character similar to that period of cruelty, then they do not suffer from this sensitive nervous system. But this man is suffering from it through certain events in his life which roused a deeply buried complex.

I am now beginning to see the record of this cruelty. It goes back a hundred years or so. It is difficult to get the exact time. This man's ancestors moved from the south to a cold northern country. Life was hard there. But the B's, as we will call them, were content with little so long as they might live in peace. They had been driven by wars to the north. They were austere, ascetic people with a high code of morals. One of them married a beautiful Jewess. This man B. was devoted to her and they had one son. These three with B.'s old father, were all the world to each other.

Unfortunately his beautiful wife was admired by a Russian, a high official in the town in which they lived. He made advances to her which were rejected with anger and contempt. The Russian was infuriated and became offensive. B. struck him because he was insulting his wife. The Russian had a sadistic nature of a type that is slow but utterly cruel in its vengeance.

He made representations to the authorities against the Jews of the town and a pogrom was organized. One night the ghetto was fired. The whole community of the Jews, as the Russian told the beautiful Jewess, were to suffer for her and her husband's offence. But the worst punishment was allotted to them. In her own and her young son's presence the hands of her husband and her father were hacked off. The women were driven out into the night and the snow. Then in the presence of the terrified son the Russian violated his mother.

Later their own people tried to help this unfortunate family. But after much awful suffering the two men died.

The Jewess survived, but became insane. She lived until her son was about eighteen. But this appalling experience of his made of him a nervous wreck. This experience became a part of the subconscious mind which was passed on to subsequent generations. Until recent times they lived in fear of persecution, or were persecuted. So the complex sown in the subconscious did not fade out. However, in the last forty or fifty years times were better for them. The complex remained deeply buried and might never have been roused if it had not been for certain events in this man's life. I allude to the man who owns the pen. When he was a tiny child, probably before he can remember, a brother of his or someone nearly related, cut his hand badly and he was very frightened by the sight of the blood and the child's cries. It was to a small child, a mere baby, very terrifying. So the experience was repressed, buried and forgotten by his conscious mind. Later this brother, or near relation, died. This death was another experience associated with darkness and terror.

It happened quite a long time after the episode of the cut hand—years after. But the two were linked together and they bore a resemblance to the complex of the severed hands, and subsequent death of the two male ancestors, also to the darkness of insanity that came over the mind of the woman in that generation.

The owner of the pen, when a man, had worry over loss in work I think. I see some worry about work. He took up some new work that had to do with fire. Fire was again associated with the night when the ghetto was fired, the night of unforgettable horror, the memory of which was in his subconscious mind.

As a result, when this man's hand was injured the complex produced nervous illness as well. The man, who is very gifted, is capable of going far in life if he will

CASE XII

realize what is handicapping him and that it belongs to the
past and is dead and done with, therefore it has no real
power over him.   That is if he exerts his mind and will and
says to himself that he will not allow this fantasy of horror
and terror, this irrational thing, to conquer him.

He can cure himself if he will face and realize the cause.
He is a sane, normal man who is merely the victim of his
racial past, which he can in time dismiss by breaking
through its entanglements.   It would, of course, be a good
thing for him if he could obtain other work which would
give more scope for his excellent abilities.   Work not connected with fire.   But at present that may not be possible.

Do not tell the patient, but it may well be a difficult
case to cure owing to the tragic character of the past and
the links of experience in his own life—there are the
precious hands, the loss of which destroyed all power to
work and live, for those two ancestors."

A study of this narrative led to the collection of further
information of some collateral interest.

(1) The family involved in the story came to X—from
Riga, in Latvia, about fifty or sixty years ago.   This was
evidently that cold northern country mentioned in the
the narrative, and the period of time quoted corresponded
with known facts.

(2) That the emigration of this family followed persecution, or the fear of it, can be inferred.   More than twenty
years ago, an old Jew, a contemporary of the first X—,
ancestor of the patient, informed the writer that in his
youth he remembered seeing the Cossack cavalry charging
through his native village, spearing the children as they
went.   They were the Gestapo of that country and that
period.

(3) That two million Jews in Europe, according to
official estimates, have been exterminated in the last four

years by methods of unparalleled ferocity is further proof
that the fear was well founded. (In Latvia I am informed
that they have been exterminated completely. Their
number there had been about thirty-five thousand.)

(4) A friend, a contemporary of the patient, gave the
information that other members of his family were even
more highly strung and unstable than the patient. He
related also that when they were growing up together a
Jew who lived in a contiguous house cut his hand and died
in a few days of tetanus or septicaemia. The author
remembered this case. This tragedy made a profound
impression on the whole small Jewish community living
in that locality. It might well be the death referred to in
the record.

(5) That prior to joining the fire brigade the patient
had had temporary employment in a cement factory. That
he had obtained compensation when his eye had been
burnt by lime. At that time he had not been in the least
disturbed by the consequent danger to his sight. Nevertheless he broke down later over a quite trivial accident to
this hand. This fact is of considerable collateral interest.

The essence of this story, then, correlates in an extraordinary manner a suppositious history of severed hands
and the firing of a ghetto, a juvenile experience of severe
hand injuries in others and an adult experience of hand
injury associated again with fire to the patient himself. A
cruel series of coincidences, let it be supposed.

Further confirmation of the truth of such a story cannot
be obtained. But one can hardly regard it as pure
imagination or ingenious fabrication on the part of the
sensitive. Moreover, such experiences must be very
numerous in the recent horror in Europe, let alone the past.
A retired colonel, a friend of the writer, informed him that
during the retreat from Belgium in the First World War

he had personally witnessed a German soldier deliberately sever both hands from a Belgian boy with his bayonet and mutilate a nun who had attempted to prevent this brutal act. The colonel shot the man and then reported the matter (reversing the procedure that should have been adopted). Severing the hands appears to be a widely recognized and long-established indulgence of sadists.

To return to the case history:

The patient had the story and its implications fully explained to him and he was enjoined never to think of them, as they had lost all power over him. This was emphasized and reiterated and formed the " motive " of his psychological treatment.

His entire acceptance of the story as it was unfolded to him was so complete that it almost conveyed the illusion of recounting a previous familiar experience to an individual. His subconscious memory appeared to affirm its absolute truth to him. Thus a tangible, reasonable cause that could be combated was substituted in place of a vague and therefore menacing and overmastering fear. As a result he rapidly recovered his confidence: he ceased altogether and at once to worry about his hand. Circumstances have compelled him to continue his occupation. He is diligently searching for a different outlet for his abilities. He has thrice called, when on leave, to express his gratitude embarrassingly and affirm his recovery.

This narrative, it is submitted, justifies the assumption that in assessing the actions of others the memories handed down to them from the past should be investigated and appraised before any final judgment can be passed on them.

The fears, the persecutions, the nights of horror, the torture chambers, the silent graves of friends and relatives unjustly slain—any such experiences from the life adventures of ancestors could undoubtedly extend their influence out of the past and affect the actions of descendants in the present, particularly if such descendants suffered from a minor shock or trauma of an analogous nature. Thus an act of cowardice, as it is popularly conceived, may well have been initiated by some terrible and insistent urge out of the forgotten past which, unknown and unexplained, has condemned many a man to the opprobrium of his fellows.

The psychological as well as the physical attributes are inherited, modified or aggravated, as each generation passes, according as the genes that carry them are dominant or recessive. Terrors, quite incomprehensible to some of us, have their roots nourished by forgotten horrors. Dead hands stretch out of the past and mould the present. Into the future they extend their clutching fingers and twist and distort our decisions and destinies.

A wise man, then, should be slow to judge, slower still to condemn. Nor is it wise to probe too deeply into the tragic past or the still more tragic present, which hangs like a thundercloud over the people of the Jewish race.

Much have they suffered, greatly are they to be pitied, and in our judgment of their actions never should they be condemned hastily, nor should their great services to our civilization ever be forgotten.

One cannot contemplate the present agony of the human race without endeavouring to assess some of its consequences in connection with the generations that are yet to come. After the first world war the writer assisted a male child into the world, whose father had just returned from nine months of work in a German coalmine. He had been a prisoner of war. During the period he was in a coalmine he never saw daylight; suffered unspeakably, physically and emotionally; fear haunted him. Until his

94

son reached the age of 10 years the son had such a horror
of all visitors that he always hid under a bed or a table when
strangers came and whenever the doctor was called. His
illnesses were nightmares to both. He was born with a
terrible fear complex dominant, and even now, 29 years
later, and in spite of the most careful upbringing, he has a
haunted look. A daughter born four years later took after
the mother and had no such heritage.

Ten years later the father himself consulted the writer.
He stated that he found that when acting as church warden,
and handing round the plate for collection, he found himself staggering and dizzy. It was explained to him that
he was going back in his mind, and reliving his experience
in the coal mine, where he had worked with a Russian, he
recovered completely.

What of the children of the men of this last and in
many ways the most ghastly of all wars, or of the civilians
who had survived the unspeakable horrors of the bombing,
the air raid shelters, the concentration and extermination
camps of Europe, where human suffering reached its
ultimate peak? What of their descendants?

Perhaps it is a matter for thankfulness that they will
become the care of other generations of physicians whose
outlook will have widened with the passage of time, and
who will have an increasing appreciation and a deeper
insight into the problems and implications of psychological
heredity.

CASE XIII. A STUDY IN CHILD PSYCHOLOGY

THE difficulties in dealing with neuroses in childhood
vary considerably from those met with in adults. In
the adult the character is defined, the personality fixed. In
the child the character is only developing, the personality

is ill defined and changing; further, the child is more vulnerable in every respect. A child shows more susceptibility to suggestions than an adult, so that greater delicacy and care must be employed in utilising them on his behalf. One therefore approaches his psychological study with some apprehension.

The father of the small boy whose case is herewith presented sought advice in the psychological treatment and upbringing of his son.

He was seven years old, and it had been noticed for some time past that he had been manifesting an unusual degree of nervousness. He had established the habit of biting his nails on the slightest provocation when strangers appeared, or when he became excited or frightened, or any occasion that might promote the slightest nervous tension. His nails had been bitten down to the roots; besides the objectionable nature of the habit, it seemed to suggest that some nervous factors were at work; these the father wished if possible to overcome.

The boy had been involved in a severe night air raid at the age of three years. On this occasion he had been assured, whenever he awoke, that the noises and explosions were due to the milk trains; he did not appear to be frightened, he returned to sleep and seemed to accept the explanation. He was taken to his home on the following day, and the subject had never again been referred to.

When he was little over a year old he had received two inoculations against diphtheria. He seemed to have become unduly nervous and frightened of his medical attendant as a result of this experience.

These were the only two incidents in his life that could in any way be regarded as in a measure responsible for initiating the nervous habits.

It was clear that in such a case a treatment by painting his fingers with some distasteful substance, or the wearing of cotton gloves, would not of themselves prove adequate. It was thought by the author, who was his medical attendant, that some incident in his race history might be exerting its influence on the boy's temperament and that its investigation might throw some light on the matter.

It was thought that it might not be easy for a sensitive to visualize incidents in this child's race history owing to his being only seven years old. It was therefore decided to investigate the racial history and character of both parents in addition. A fountain-pen was obtained from the father, a worn glove from the mother and a school cap from the small boy.

These objects were sent to the sensitive and the information was given (1) That the family was of the Jewish race. (2) That the father was a solicitor, a self-made man of great ability and rising reputation, and a friend and patient of the author. (3) That the mother was stated to have considerable musical and artistic gifts and was probably somewhat highly strung. (4) The story of the small boy was given and his nervous disability described, the air raid was mentioned, but the incident of the inoculation was not referred to as it was not regarded as of sufficient significance. (5) It was stated that in the author's opinion the boy was of unusual intelligence, with a most attractive child personality.

The sensitive was asked to investigate any particulars that could be discovered in the race history of the group bearing on the boy's nervous condition, a knowledge of which might be helpful in his treatment.

The sensitive had never met or seen the three individuals concerned and knew nothing further about them.

G

The following records were obtained:

(1) THE FATHER OF THE BOY

"The owner of this pen is of unusual interest partly because of what he represents. In the pool of his race memory is the ancient symbol of the tabernacle. This has a peculiar significance. It means that in the distant past ancestors of his were the elect people of a chosen tribe. To express it in terms of a later period they were revered by their own people, as in other nations kings were revered, when the divine right of kings was recognized. But this man's ancestors never reigned as kings. In that far past I write of they were set apart to serve as priests of bodily and spiritual health, as law-givers. They handled and used sacred emblems, gold ornaments, connected with their religion. It was the supreme privilege, and they had to be worthy. For in the eyes of their people they were second to God. God spoke through them on rare occasons, it was believed.

There is a material kingship, a kingship of lands; but there is a kingship of the spirit which was valued more by this man's nation than the material lordship. I am not using extravagant terms when I say that certain of this man's ancestors many hundred of years ago were rulers of the Kingdom of the Spirit among their own people. So he is of royal blood. This man should be proud of his origin, for such rulers had to be true, strong, just, honest, intellectually and spiritually, as well as in the material sense. All these qualities were necessary to those through whom God might speak. In the days of the dispersion and the scattering of the nation of the Jews the Gs' were in several countries. For a time they lived in Russia, at a later period in Germany. A few were for a short time in Holland and Belgium. Generations of them had to endure the cruel and limiting laws of the Gentiles. There was for them a period of great hardship and persecution in Germany.

The name G—was given them by their own people, not because they were jewellers—though some of them did follow that trade, but because they were associated with the sacred emblems of their own people's faith. Thy had charge of these gold ornaments in times of persecution. It placed them in a highly honoured position—the highest, in fact, in the eyes of their people; but it also placed them in a position of great peril.

Their Gentile persecutors were aware of the existence of these gold ornaments, and, greedy for wealth, used to torture and persecute in their search for them. The Gs'. through their fine spiritual heritage, developed an extraordinary strength of character, a purposefulness which preserved them from any breakdown of a nervous or mental character—a breakdown that would have been the certain result, to more ordinary people, if they had been subjected to the ordeals they endured in order to preserve what was holy and sacred: the mystical symbols of their nation's faith. Furthermore, in those earlier times, as keepers of the people's religious emblems, they became inbued with faith to a high degree. They were God-fearing people; that is to say they only feared God and not man. They feared only lest they should fail Him. This fearlessness as regards man, and their faith in the Highest, were so burning and so sincere that they overcame any neurotic disturbances that might have arisen, should have arisen, through the persecution and contempt of the Gentiles. So, unlike many Jews, the owner of this pen has no neurasthenic tendencies.

Now let us take the later history of his race. There came a time when the treasure and tradition were gone. The family belonged to a terribly poor community oppressed by harsh laws. Then their strong purposefulness, developed as Keepers of the Holy Treasure, as guardians of a mythical faith, had to be concentrated on the mere struggle to survive. It developed into an almost obsessional craving for work, a subtle and quick brain because opportunities were so poor, the difficulties so many. From this period this man has derived a remarkable capacity for hard work and an understanding of the poor man and his problems. But he is tolerant and takes broad, not narrow, views, because in that far past his ancestors belonged to a spiritual aristocracy. Then, as leaders of the people, they had to plan, think and act for the people, so his views are not narrow and individualistic. As regards his faults, his tendency is to overwork his quick clever brain on one line. Too great purposefulness may in time narrow his activities, to the detriment of his psychological and possibly his bodily health. He should vary his activities more than he does, else he may become drained nervously as he grows older and resistance lessens.

Physical exercise should not be neglected, and there should be some out-of-door interest, or cultural interest, as relaxation. Again, he is in the aristocratic tradition in being a very proud man. So he must not let himself be too much hurt if anyone he is fond of falls below the standard in success and morals he expects from them. He is an optimist because of that inner faith of the tabernacle which has never died. Moods of despondency would only come through too much brainwork, or through an invasion of the racial memory—pessimism. For most of his people had every justification for taking the worst view of human nature owing to the racial past. I have only given a rough outline of this past history in order to show how the character-structure was built up.

The most beautiful as well as the most ugly inclinations of man result from the long social process which in each generation creates man. But because for many generations they were in this case law-givers, leaders of their fellows, the later more deteriorating character of the social process had no effect on what was already fundamental in their nature. The interest in spiritual things in modern times faded. This man has great business ability, also ambition. He is not intuitive, he reasons everything out. He has a fine streak of generosity and is determined and go-ahead.

He is honest and well balanced, consistent, fluent. The source of these qualities lies in the far past of his race. In his own profession he will go as far as is possible. In a big city in England he would have done exceedingly well. For his honesty, great capacity, in a country where there are greater opportunities, would have led to considerable wealth and power. But here, where there is a narrower scope, he is less likely quickly to wear himself out. He is fundamentally an aristocrat in character and may well be proud of those ancestors of his who were leaders of their own people.''

(2) THE MOTHER AND THE SMALL BOY

'' The owner of this glove is a highly civilized type of human being. The artistic and musical gifts are combined in her to a considerable degree. For these she has to pay through her nerves being tuned up to concert pitch. At one time her people were in Russia and Poland. This race experience has left the most marked impression on the race character for two reasons.

(1) : it led to the development of the artistic and musical perceptions; (2): her family lived in ghettos for a time, and never knew when their homes might be plundered and burned.

Long ago some of her people experienced, on two occasions, nights of horror when they were driven from their dwellings and the elders of the family were wounded and killed, the women outraged, all their possessions stolen and they were turned adrift to starve. Now this all links up with the little boy whose cap I sense. I will show later how it has already affected him. He is the most remarkable of these three people. He has his mother's sensitive perceptions, her artistic and musical gifts, also her highly strung nervous system. But he has his father's ability, clever brain and capacity for action. That capacity could be stultified, his energies paralysed, if his nervous system was put to any great strain, if he was discouraged or frightened by some bullying influence. His father's attitude towards him is of the first importanc. He should be tender and kind and encouraging to him in every way. The boy will need every encouragement. He must not be over-indulged, spoiled or petted. But his father should never by any acts arouse a father-fear in the boy's subconscious mind. It is important that there should be a relationship of complete confidence between these two. It is important not merely for his own sake, but because given favourable conditions this boy could develop into a remarkable man who contributes much of service to the community through his great gifts.

Already there is an active complex in his unconscious mind. It links up with the scene of night and terror that made such a marked impression on his mother's race memory. It was unfortunate that when he was very young he had the experience of an air raid at night. To the ordinary observer his consciousness was not in any way affected by this episode, and that is a correct view to take. But the subconsciousness between the ages of one and five is to a great extent in control of the individual. It is acutely affected by any great danger when there is a highly strung nervous system to record the impression made. The subconscious mind of a small child will record danger and the fears of adults around him to an extreme degree, even when the child is asleep, or dozing, in a number of cases. For the conscious mind is undeveloped, so it puts no barrier between, as in the case of older people. An unbearable feeling of aloneness and insignificance was roused in the boy's unconsciousness from its source—that ancestral experience in that eastern town, during the air-raid night when he was only about three years old. Later it produced a certain masochistic element.

When an individual is driven by an unbearable feeling of aloneness and insignificance, he attempts to overcome it by getting rid of his 'self' (all this takes place in the unconscious); his way to achieve this riddance is to suffer, to make himself insignificant. This boy's habit of biting his nails is an expression of that subconscious attitude. But pain and suffering are not what he wants, he has really a great dread of them. But if the complex gets hold of him he is like a moth drawn to a candle-flame. He seeks what he fears most.

However, given favourable conditions this boy's complex will not be of a serious character, though it is so far answerable for a high degree of nervousness. Another element in this complex is that his mother's people were stabbed by weapons used by their persecutors, in those raid nights of their dwellings long ago. It seems this little boy had a needle stuck into him by a doctor when he was young. This experience connected him with that racial memory also. He has an unreasonng fear of illness which is associated wth pain. His physician can help him to overcome this by making the boy familiar with him as a friend. With the physican as his friend it will seem to the subconscious that there is nothing to be afraid of any more.

He becomes his defender against the soldier and is no longer the soldier who stabbed him so cruelly with a weapon, that led his ancestor in the past to bleed to death. A physician who shows interest in this boy's interest, who is socially a friend as well as a medical adviser, will be of real help in overcoming the irrational fear of pain and illness latent in the subconscious mind of the child.

The boy's father can do much to overcome, and may in time completely destroy, the air-raid impression. The boy then felt utterly insignificant and alone, deserted by his all- protecting father, who seemed to be unable to help at that time.

To rectify this the father must not belittle the boy, make him feel insignificant and alone again by sarcasm, or sterness, or ridicule. The father must make his son feel that he believes in his high capabilities. He should applaud his little successes in school. He should make him feel that he knows he has it in him to be an important and successful man. The word encouragement is the keynote to sound in the case of this highly sensitive child. Comfort and not rebuke should be given when the boy has failures. His mother should encourage and develop the boy's artistic and musical sensibilities.

At the same time don't let the boy overwork, don't press him too hard on the mental side.   Let there be a certain balance in his life, an outlet in physical and out-of-door activities. To strengthen the nervous system the physical development must be carefully attended to. It is likely, as happens in most schools, that the boy may meet with bullies. To counteract their influence the father should give his son a proper pride in himself and his family. The fact that his ancestors were aristocrats and leaders of their own people in the far past should be imparted to him; that he is never inferior, he is the equal, and more than the equal, in what matters of those contemporary to him. Thus much may be done to eradicate the subconscious feeling of insignificance and helplessness which produces this nervousness, of which there have been signs already in the boy.

Carefully handled by his father and mother and given every opportunity for development, he should go far indeed, and, provided the opportunities are there, might at a later date make his mark on his age. At least he should succeed in whatever line he takes up; for he has so much latent ability. The only danger is any nervous conflict that would paralyse energy. And this will not occur if he is encouraged, strengthened and stimulated in the manner suggested and if his adult contacts, that is to say his love-life, when he is a man, are fortunate."

Mr. G—has given confirmation of the essential points of the record.

He states that his family belonged to the priestly tribe and were descendants of Aaron. There is no written proof of this, but the tradition of origin is recognised; and amongst Hebrews he is known as a "Cohen," which is the Hebrew equivalent of the English word "priest." His wife similarly belongs to the tribe of Levi, who were designated to serve the priests in the Temple.

With reference to the possession of gold ornaments connected with religious ceremonies, this again is of the traditional past. Mr. G's father had informed him that his family possessed a gold "pushka," or box, richly chased, which had been handed down for generations. It was said to contain family papers. When he left Lithuania at the age of fifteen years the box was left with relatives. It is possible this may have been originally a temple treasure.

He knew that his forbears had come through France, Belgium, Holland, Germany and Russia (Lithuania).

His wife's family came from a Polish-Russian border town. He connects his family movement to Russia from Germany to a mass migration of Jews from Bohemia some hundreds of years ago owing to harsh anti-Semitic legislation. So far as he knew, his family name of G— had no religious or other significance. About a hundred years ago, when conscription was imposed in Lithuania, if there was only one son he was excused from service. Many Jewish families avoided conscription by giving different surnames to their sons. In his family seven different names were assumed at that time.

He recorded an interesting trait in his own character that has an indirect bearing on the record given, that as guardian of the sacred emblems his family lived in peril. Mr. G— is roused instantly by the slightest disturbance in his house and from the deepest sleep, and he immediately comes to complete consciousness. This is not due to sound transmission, for he is completely deaf in his left ear owing to a radical mastoid operation in childhood. He sleeps with his left ear uppermost, the sound ear muffled in the pillow. Nevertheless the faintest intruding evidence of human presence brings him into instant consciousness. He feels as if a thread were broken or a button pressed in his mind calling him to action.

As guardian of the sacred treasures the G's through generations would no doubt at all times, sleeping or waking, have been keenly and constantly on the alert.

All of these facts Mr. G. states are purely personal and private knowledge, and could not have become known to the sensitive by any ordinary means. In reviewing this case:

(1) It is to be noted that the sensitive has drawn

attention to the fact that an incident of major importance
was the diptheria inoculation. This was performed with
a fine hypodermic needle (two doses of A.P.T.), at the age
of about a year and a half. This, in the sensitive's view,
became symbolically identical in the child's subconscious
mind with the race memory of the stabbings of ancestors
in a ghetto—an incident of horror and fear.

The information of the inoculation had not been given
to the sensitive, yet she succeeded in perceiving it, and
furthermore ascribed a significance to it which the author
had not contemplated.

On reconsidering the incident he recalls that the
second inoculation was only accomplished with a flood of
tears and exaggerated manifestation of fear on the part of
the little boy.

Moreover, when a mild attack of measles occurred
some years later his visits were received with tears and
commotion by the patient, and much assurance was
necessary on each occasion that no puncture with a needle
was contemplated. (Since then the author has succeeded in
establishing a more friendly relationship with the small boy
and they have at least reached the stage of armed
neutrality).

(2) The importance is emphasised, in studying the
psychology of a child, of including an investigation of the
parents' personalities and their race history.

A child personality will become a varying amalgam
of two characters: in this case diverse—the one purposeful,
able and determined, the other artistic, musical and highly
strung. Further, the building up of the structure of these
two personalities is indicated by the sensitive, by references
to the complex social forces out of the past which played
their part in moulding them.

Thus we have (1) great business capacity and energy, and (2) high artistic gifts, merging together in the son—an unusual combination with noticeable potentialities.

On the other hand, it is clearly suggested that the whole potential personality of the child could be marred and stultified by the incidents of fear, introduced in the first instance by brutal murders in a ghetto, and later activated and reinforced by (1) the use of a hypodermic needle; (2) by the accident of an air raid.

(3) The very great impressionability of the child's subconscious mind is shown in the first eight or ten years, before the barriers of the conscious mind are built up. The child may pass through an air raid oblivious apparently to its horrors and dangers, its explosions and its noises, but a lasting impression of paralysing fear may have been inscribed on his subconscious mind.

It is not too much to suggest that the alphabet of the future personality of the adult is stamped on the vulnerable and plastic subconscious mind of the child in the first eight or ten years.

It is therefore of real importance that the human and psychic contacts during this period of a child's life should be subject for careful reflection as each year passes. Among these contacts the mother comes first. At a certain stage her attitude towards her son is vital. She is the infant's first protector, his source of warmth and food to whom he instinctively turns.

If a nurse is employed her disposition should be carefully considered. Such an employee usually lives and sleeps in the room with the child. It is as important that she should not be cruel, thoughtless or hasty, disciplining the child by fear rather than justice, as it is, for example, that she should not suffer from chronic catarrh, oral sepsis, or recurrent tonsilitis.   On the one hand the child could be brought up in an atmosphere of harshness, injustice and fear; on the other he could be condemned to live and sleep in an atmosphere continually reinforced and supercharged with pneumococcus, streptococcus viridans or streptococcus haemolyticus. Either case would be equally reprehensible and fraught with both psychic and physical dangers that need not be enumerated.

The influence of the father increases as the child personality commences to unfold and crystallize; in this particular child, owing to the age and sex and the stage he has reached, it becomes paramount.

(4) The psychological suggestions made by the sensitive for the father on the importance of his attitude to the growing child should therefore prove most helpful in his treatment, as they are based on a careful analysis of the two primary personalities from which, blended together, the embryonic personality of the child is in the process of being built.

It may be urged that the recommendations for treatment go no further than a common-sense analysis and appraisal of the case by an expert would yield.   On the other hand, it is doubtful whether any expert could obtain so comprehensive a basis on which to build the foundation for his recommendations for treatment.

It has been thought advisable to include this case because its research throws some valuable light on child psychology and the investigation of the causes of some of the neuroses that may be initiated during that period.

Ten years later the boy has completely recovered and is progressing favourably in all other aspects (education games etc.).

CASE XIV. A CASE EXHIBITING INHIBITION OF CONCENTRATION

THE patient was a medical student of Jewish nationality, twenty-five years of age. He had passed his first three medical examinations brilliantly; but, having reached this point in his medical career, he had failed to continue his studies. He stated that he was unable to continue to concentrate his mind on his work, and he had lost two years. This check had caused the greatest anxiety to his parents. He was persuaded, with considerable difficulty, to consult the writer.

He was found to be of fine physique, he enjoyed good health, and gave the impression of very great mental ability. His demeanour was composed, his manner and conversation were mature and cultured, and he showed little or no sign of embarrassment when his disability was discussed. He stated that all his interests were medical and scientific, particularly in its more recent advances, and he was anxious to be able to carry on research himself. He stated that he had lost all power of concentration, but could advance no reason for this, nor would he accept any of the suggestions as to the causes that were advanced tentatively. He realized fully the importance of his qualification, to himself and to his parents.

He realized that he could not continue his own interest in research until he had qualified, but though he had been able without the slightest difficulty to concentrate on the subjects of his first three examinations, pursuing them far further than was necessary, so that he found the most difficult questions trivial and easy, yet he could not now concentrate his mind in any manner on his final subjects.

This was the kernel of his difficulty and no explanation was offered or discovered.

CASE XIV

It was suggested to him that a cause for his trouble lay probably in his race inheritance. His race's history, including its tragic recent experiences, were discussed fully, and their consequences for the individual considered. The subject of psychological inheritance was illustrated. He was shown how it could influence action, and how such actions could be investigated and analysed by means of ESP. His interest was finally captured, and when he was made to realize that his disability might be overcome by these means he asked to have the matter enquired into.

His fountain-pen was sent to the sensitive with the main particulars contained in the information already given. She was asked to search for the causes of the psycho-neurosis, the existence of which was suspected. The sensitive's record is as follows:

"The owner of this pen is of great interest, because there are in him remarkable potentialities. He has a fine brain, and he has the rare gift of being capable of original thought. Later, when he is older and has more experience, he would be capable of making his mark in medical research, or he would be successful in the initiation of new treatments. With such a brain he could in time become a leader in his profession, or indeed in any scientific line he studied; that is, if he could overcome a cumulative anxiety-complex, which lies in his unconscious mind. Like the huge stump of a very ancient tree, it has many roots. These come from unfortunate experiences, mostly connected with persecution, with the brutality of mobs, with, in short, the Gentile nation which hemmed in the little community to which his ancestors belonged. This community might be likened to that of a fortress which was frequently besieged. The defenders were anxious, always afraid of another attack from an alien world. Constantly therefore on the alert, they developed (1) a highly sensitive physical nervous system, (2) an anxiety-complex.

This man's physical nervous system is capable of putting out a greater effort than the average nervous system, but it is more easily exhausted; and then only complete mental relaxation and life in the open air in quiet country can initiate its recovery.

But at present this very able young man is suffering from a discharge that emanates from the anxiety-complex in his unconscious mind, which is part of the race mind.

For centuries, owing to persecutions, his family living in that small community always lived in a thoroughly justified fear of the great world. The Gentiles who represented the great world were like some huge and pitiless monster, aganist whom there was no defence once it was roused.

This young man will have to go out into the great world to earn his living in a year's time if he passes his final examination. So far he has been training as a student, in other words living safely within his community. His subconscious mind, filled with the ancient fear of the hostile, persecuting world I have described as the monster, is set on preventing his having to face it. The complex of fear of the men of Bohemia who robbed and beat up his family, and of the people of another nation who did likewise, paralyses his will, makes it impossible for him to concentrate. People who speak German, their native tongue, were particularly brutal to his ancestors.

But he will escape from having to face this nightmare monster if he is unable to go for his exam. The monster, the modern world is absolutely harmless in this country. But the subconscious mind is quite irrational when ruled by a deeply rooted fear, the sum total of generations of fear. It assumes a hostility is waiting there for it, a hostility which is not there.

When a schoolboy, the patient was unkindly treated on more than one occasion by bullying school-fellows. The fact that he was a Jew led to their cowardly attacks when he was young. He has probably forgotten these incidents, because anything that rouses a latent ancestral fear in a small child's mind is usually repressed from the conscious memory because it is unpleasant and unbearable to think of. This repression is harmful. It gave the ancient racial complex life and power to influence the patient's mentality in later years, when some stress or anxiety gave it an opportunity to manifest itself.

It should be noted that a number of Jews who do not develop any neurosis as a result of the anxiety-persecution-complex are those of average capacity or those who in early life do not experience any alarming or onerous shocks that correspond in character to the racial complex. Men with special gifts, like the patient, are far more open to its influence.

The patient resembles in many respects an ancestor of his, a young man who lived on the borders of Russia. His time had come to serve as a Russian soldier. He was proud and hated what the Russians did to his people, and was determined therefore not to be their conscripted slave. He hid in a forest for a time. His people protected him, bringing him food, but eventually he was captured. His punishment for evading military conscription was so severe that he was ruined mentally and physically. One of the most brilliant and promising of the young men of his tribe, he became a wreck, and his talents and life were wholly wasted. He added to the racial complex his experience—more particularly of those days when he hid in the forest.

H

Controlled by this episode, which links up with the small, comparatively trivial episode, of the bullying schoolboys in the present life, this patient is now living in that forest. His unconscious mind forces the consciousness to remain inert; so that he may not have to go out into the hostile world. By inhibiting his capacity for concentration, it seeks to prevent him taking his degree, and thus he is kept in safety at home. The world to the unconscious seems especially hostile now, as the Germans were brutal torturers of his race, and the German military menace at the present time looms large on the horizon of the mind.

The instinct of self-preservation therefore insists on seclusion in the forest.

The patient, when he realizes that he is the victim of experiences that are past and therefore dead, will be able to recover his capacity for concentration; that is, if he makes a determined use of his excellent reasoning powers and banishes this nightmare of the past which holds him paralysed in its grip. It would be helpful for him for a few days to make himself tired with fresh air and exercise and give his brain a rest for a short time from the tension of the cruel conflict it has been experiencing. Let him after resolving this complex and after a brief interlude of physical exertion in the open air, start work, for he should then be able to concentrate with all his old brilliant capacity.

The doctor might consider giving him some tonic, which might stimulate and nourish nervous system and brain. It would be helpful as an additional auto-suggestion rather than for its properties as a drug.''

In due course this explanation was read to the patient, and he was enjoined to realize it fully. His failure to concentrate was due entirely to experiences out of a past that has terminated.* He must not allow the past to influence his present or his future, adversely.

Details of the advice given was of a similar nature to that employed in former cases. He followed this advice, and three weeks later he reported that he was able again to concentrate and was now accomplishing ten hours a day of study.

While the case still remains under treatment and may require further psychological assistance, an encouraging start has been made. After two years' inhibition, capacity for concentration of the mind has returned. It is possible that the subconscious mind may lead the patient to wander into higher branches of medical thought to the neglect of examination essentials, and thereby elude the immediate pressing examination problem. But a satisfactory start has been made, and with guidance may lead to his ultimate complete recovery.

It is worth noting the following points when comment is made on this case.

The more brilliant the potential endowments of a central nervous system the more sensitive it becomes. In the environment, education and upbringing of individuals with such nervous systems unusual care should be exercised if the maximum benefit to the community is to be obtained from their services.

A cherished orchid requires special attention if its bloom is to be brought to perfection. Instruments of precision have to be sheltered and kept in exact order if their delicate contribution to science are to continue unimpaired. How much more so is this the case with the human machine.

* This patient's ancestors lived among Germans and Russians for a considerable period in their racial history. Some of them were conscripted for military service in Russia.

The ultimate history of the case is submitted. A younger brother became a barrister. Together they took part in a journalistic venture. Five years later medicine was recommended, and the final examination passed without difficulty by the patient.

A curious sequel to this case may be added though it has only an indirect bearing on it. It concerns the faculty of ESP.

The writer received a charming letter of thanks to both the sensitive and himself from this patient, so charming was the letter that he enclosed it in a sealed envelope and sent it to the sensitive suggesting that she should investigate it by ESP without opening it. This she did in the presence of a witness. The result throws some light on the faculty of ESP, it indicates that the more recent, more intense and more emotional impressions, are the most easily picked up. This was her report:—

" It is difficult to read this record, I do not feel through the wrapping any strong emanation. It may be that this envelope prevents me making a contact. I get the impression of a man who is over fifty, and he talks rather as a man over seventy, he assumes this attitude, it is a subconscious pose. His vibrations are coming to me now. He has considerable ability and a probing imagination, sometimes his imagination carries him beyond what is reasonable, but it is useful in thought occasionally to out-distance reason. He seems to be in and out of peoples' houses—he pays visits—he is interested in a branch of science—medical science, but he likes best its obscure aspects. He is not very interested in the humdrum routine of medicine, he should be working in medical research.

I cannot get away from his vibrations. He has some anxiety about a woman, who is dear to him, he tries to suppress this anxiety and this is not good for him, he should face it.   He is inclined temperamentally to be a pessimist, this is a pity with his ability and knowledge.   I find these vibrations from this man and a feeling is now emerging, a desire to know the fate or future of the woman he is anxious about, it is her bad health, he wants to know whether she will die suddenly.   So far as I can see she carries on better than he anticipates and years' of companionship lie ahead of these two, that is the secret intimate thought in the man's mind, I mean this fear which is partly suppressed about this woman and her future, it is of an emotional character and prevents me getting anything else from this envelope.   He must be reassured on this point about this woman; if he is, then he will be better in every respect, and less liable to this anxiety. This is all I can see about this anxiety, but this man is an interesting mixture of the saint and the scientist.''

In this case the sensitive gave an accurate account of the author's own mental condition. He had written on the outside of the envelope, further, a letter from him to the sensitive had enclosed the envelope.   In consequence of these mistakes in ESP technique, the envelope was saturated with the emanations or vibrations (so-called) of the author, and as the sensitive disclosed, he was most anxious about his wife. She had had one severe stroke, and during eleven long years a further stroke was anticipated from day to day. She had two further minor strokes during this period and three heart attacks, before a final stroke terminated her life. She survived the above writing for about six years, a far longer period than the author anticipated. It was a time of great anxiety to him, as was indicated in the sensitive's note.

CASE XV. AN ANXIETY NEUROSIS

IN the previous case it was observed how an anxiety neurosis overcame an individual at the commencement of his career, almost before it had begun. In this case the patient was able to fight his psychological disability right through his life until he was a little over 60 years of age, when it overcame him.

He was a Scotsman of small build but vigorous frame. He was an engineer and had had a successful and distinguished career. He had worked in Burma and had taken part in the construction of the great road from its inception. He had traversed the whole area of its layout when it was unexplored jungle. During the whole period he had worked and played with intense activity, even organising Rugby football in the tropics, which he indulged in up to his thirty-fifth year. He suffered no very serious tropical illness and enjoyed good health during the whole period, during the greater part of which he was accompanied by his wife. He was proud of his unusual activity and health. He had no family. He returned to this country when his work terminated and immediately applied his constructive abilities to the engineering aspect of a shipping business and the administration of a country estate which he acquired.

During the war stresses that ensued he often continued to work night and day for several days on end, on ships that had been damaged by storm or submarine or air attack, in order to make them seaworthy as quickly as possible. After one of these experiences he developed fever. The writer was consulted for what in default of other diagnosis was labelled pyrexia of unknown origin. Search for malaria and other tropical diseases proved unsuccessful. Some septic teeth were removed with temporary benefit, but after three weeks slight nocturnal temperature continued; and at this stage pleuritic effusion appeared at the left base of his lung.   X-ray indicated a fibroid form of phthisis.   He spent six months at rest in the open air—and his lung condition became quiescent. He recommenced work under supervision.   Six months later he developed angina of effort following an attempt to lift a full crate of honey from a hive.

After three weeks' complete rest he recommenced activity at a reduced rate.

While studying a war map he suddenly became *aphasic,* partly paralysed on the *left* side and partially blind. This, it was thought, was due to a small embolus from the heart blocking a vessel in the brain.

Again his recovery was rapid.   In three weeks no symtoms remained except partial hemianopsia (half vision).   At this stage he developed a marked neurosis and fear of being alone. It became such an obsession that he passed his time consulting the eye specialist, the medical consultant, and in the intervals his wife, in almost continuous session. No amount of assurance was of more than temporary service. The sessions became longer, change of air simply increased his energy and persistence, and it became necessary for all concerned, particularly himself, that this medical persecution should be terminated.

An ESP investigation was carried out on his penknife. The sensitive was asked to endeavour to discover a cause for his immense physical and mental activity during his sixty years of life, together with the neurosis that had commenced after his third serious illness had been overcome.

Her record is as follows: October 1944.

" This is an interesting but difficult case. The individual in question has a paradoxical character. He has many fine qualities. He has been a useful worker for society. Consciously he has always been fearless. He is honest to a degree ; his word is his bond. He has fine creative capacity and constructive instincts.

He is kind ; there is no cruelty in his nature. There is only an innate tendency to be cruel to himself. He has determination and pluck, and has not during his career at any time used his gifts unworthily. But, strangely enough, though constructive and a builder for others, he has been steadily destructive as regards his own physical constitution.

He has been possessed by a feverish drive, which has led him in the past continually to overtax his body in play and work. This blind force, that springs from his unconscious mind, has never allowed him to relax sufficiently, to take things easily and lightly occasionally. He has over long periods been far too much on strain.

The origin of this feverish drive, this force, that has so used him up, may be traced to an anxiety-complex which lies in his unconscious mind. The unconscious mind, which is deeper than the subconsciousness, might be described as being also the reservoir of racial tendencies and memories. This man is the victim of his racial history. It is necessary to go a long way back into this family history in order to trace the development and growth of this racial anxiety-complex. A modern man may not be in the least pious or interested in religion, and yet he can be deeply influenced by the excessive piety and absorption in religion of long dead ancestors.

This absorption in time produces a racial type. For generations this man's ancestors were what might be described as God-fearing men. They belonged to some religious sect or Church that was Calvinistic in out-look. The calvinist's attitude was that there are those who are

CASE XV

saved and those who are destined to eternal damnation. Their fate, in this respect, was to a considerable degree determined before they were born. Thus men are created unequal, the basis of human solidarity is denied, i.e. the equality of man's fate. But over-emphasis was laid in this belief on the importance of moral effort and a virtuous life, for it was a sign that the individual belonged to the elect to be saved. Unceasing human effort was essential to salvation. The Calvinistic view of life, therefore, produced a continual state of anxiety. There was an unbearable feeling of doubt concerning one's future after death. Anyone possessed by this fear cannot relax and enjoy life, be indifferent to the future. But there was one way to escape from this unbearable feeling of uncertainty and insignificance, and that was through incessant activity. The individual had to be always doing something, to be active in order to overcome doubt and the sense of insignificance and powerlessness as regards the future. It was a force created by the conception of a God so merciless he could condemn the individual to a future of eternal fire.

This kind of continuous activity was therefore not the result of strength of character, it was a frantic escape from anxiety, for success morally, and more especially in one's work, was a sign that one was saved.

In this way a formidable anxiety-complex was created by a number of this man's ancestors. This complex produced in him the feverish drive, the blind force that led him to be so over-active during his career. Then the development through machinery of an industrial competitive society helped to increase in this man's ancestors the power of this blind force. Wealth became a virtue. For man was a mere cog in the great economic machine of society. He was important if he had capital and wholly insignificant if he had none. The machine became the master of man. In the case of this man's forebears, as in the case of many others, it increased the feeling of powerlessness and renewed and strengthened the old Calvinistic anxiety-complex which might have perished through the greater freedom of thought in modern times. Poised between great poverty and the vast fortunes made by a few, this family always felt insecure. Increasing the influence of their morbid conscience, it drove them into continual activity.

This, then, in brief, is their history. It explains the patient's excess in activity during his past life. He has now become very melancholy because physical ill-health prevents him (if he could only realize it) from indulging this anxiety-complex, this morbid conscience, by expanding himself in work and various activities to the same degree as formerly. To preserve even a small measure of physical health he will have to resolve this fantasy that originated in fear of eternal damnation in a future life and in the fear and feeling of powerlessness engendered by the economic machine of society. He is on strain all the time because of it. He must learn to relax, to take pleasure in indolence and in the little things of life.

Before closing it seems necessary to allude to another feature of his case. It is of a minor character.

There are many people whose life is related to a power outside themselves. They want to be taken care of by him or her, and they even sometimes make him responsible for the result of their own actions. Often the person does not in the least realize the fact of his dependence on another. This other is sometimes a husband, sometimes a wife, or God. The point to realize is that he is endowed by the subject's subconsciousness with magical gifts.

He or she takes away, as in the case under consideration the unconscious feeling of insecurity, the fear of aloneness. The person in this instance is the patient's wife. He requires her to spend all her time and life on him. The physical illness has helped to produce the feeling that she has the miraculous gift that gives security. He has become too dependent on her because of his inability to stand alone and face the rooted anxiety, the mysterious subconscious trouble that has induced in him deep melancholy. For now it is not possible to escape from this unconscious feeling of insecurity through constant and exhausting activities.

As this complex comes from the Unconscious, the race memory, it will be difficult for him to be convinced of it so that it may be resolved. For it is part of the fundamental racial structure. He is sane and well balanced in every other respect.

He has as well to learn to relax both mind and body to find amusement that will help him to induce relaxation. If he does not study to relax more and more, he will increase his activities which are an escape mechanism, and in so doing he will inevitably smash up his physical body.''

Treatment followed the usual lines and was rapidly successful. In his latest interview the patient stated that he considered that the terminal statement referring to his wife and the warning that she might break down nervously if he became too dependent on her was most effective in helping him back to self-control.

It is interesting to note in this case how a religion, founded on fear, can effect an individual and in fact even a whole race. " The evil that men do lives after them " ; and a religion exhorting virtue through fear of punishment can exert its baleful effect on generations unborn. It is clear that it should be replaced by one of tolerance, happiness and love.

Some years later this patient started overdoing his physical capacity. He left the Author, and was allowed, or insisted on, taking up salmon fishing. A coronary thrombosis terminated his life. The complex was too strong for him, and took its toll, when his physical powers had waned.

CASE XVI.   A CASE OF LOSS OF CONSCIOUSNESS.

THE writer was called to see Mr. R. about eleven o'clock one evening. He was in bed drinking a cup of tea, he was a vigorous, healthy man and well-known to him. The following history was given, partly by himself, partly by his wife, and later augmented by information from his friend, and through cross examination.

It was during World War II in a time of petrol shortage. He had arranged to fetch his wife who had been ill, from the extreme west of Ireland, a distance of about 200 miles.

A friend who was travelling in that direction undertook to drive him half way where he was to meet his wife ; he was then to change cars and return with her.

All went well until they neared the meeting point. Mr. R. had taken a turn at driving, they were talking about an aeroplane exhibition and a flight that Mr. R. had made. Suddenly, without warning, Mr. R. appeared to slump on the steering wheel and turned the car into the ditch, where it fell over on its side. His friend who was furthest from the door, managed to push him out, and said " Quick, Mr. R., stop that car," pointing to another drawing near. He staggered in an apparently dazed condition and "slumped" on to the road.

He remained in a more or less dazed condition until his return home with his wife in her car five or six hours later.

The following relevant history was elicited.

About ten years previously he had been run into by a motor car while riding a motor bicycle. He received a head injury and was unconscious for a week. He was three months in hospital. Shortly afterwards, while having his hair cut, his accident was mentioned, and he then suffered from what he described as a complete "black out," becoming unconscious.

He could recollect two minor attacks of faintness in the ten years that followed. On probing into his history, he recalled a football match he played in at the age fifteen, when he received a kick on the head, and found himself playing for the wrong side and remained dazed for the rest of the day.

In his childhood he remembered galloping under a tree on a pony and receiving a severe blow from a branch, on the head. During the interval between the motor bicycle accident and the present motor accident, he had driven motor cars, indulged in sports, fished, shot, etc. without any untoward happenings.

These were all the relevant facts. It appeared to be a straightforward case. There was no doubt that there was a close association in the subconscious mind between the two accidents. It was explained to him that something in the features of the road, the conversation, his anxiety about his wife, had suddenly led to a dissociation of his conscious mind, and he went back in the subconscious mind and re-lived his previous accident, even to the dazed condition that followed. He was carefully examined physically. He was assured that nothing was wrong, and the usual psychological treatment in such a case was employed. After a few days he returned to his work.

On a close analysis one cannot fail to observe, that similar accidents have occurred to others without untoward attacks of unconsciousness some years later. The writer himself suffered from a fractured skull, when nineteen years old. He was semi-conscious for over a week, and aphasic for some days, etc. He has never suffered from blackouts or fits of any sort, in his somewhat chequered subsequent forty-seven years, including war service, 1916-18, and in Ireland in the subsequent 'troubles.'

For this reason it was thought wise to reinforce the treatment if possible, by the results of an ESP investigation.

This was its contribution.

"I like the impression I receive from this object. The owner of it is a fine type of man. Loyal, straight, sincere, with a rare honesty and good mental and physical powers, he is an uncommon man in a world in which mean petty dishonesty is so prevalent. But he belongs to an old aristocratic race. I use the word 'aristocratic' in its correct sense. The true aristocratic does not stoop to do anything low, tricky or mean. His word is his bond. But he pays for being a thoroughbred by being highly strung and sensitive to impressions. This man has a good, perfectly normal brain. But there has been considerable conflict going on in his subconscious mind over a long period of years, this subconsciousness is part of the mind below consciousness, but it influences, sometimes strongly, the consciousness. His sensitiveness has left him very open to its influences, and on occasion led to his becoming unconscious.

This unconscious condition need never occur again if he properly realises its causes.

The root of it goes far back into his racial history. His people owned land and lived on it for generations. But originally a long way back, they were chiefs, rulers of their clan; people of considerable account in their own district Then they were attacked by invaders and dispossessed, they became hunted fugitives. For a very long time they led a precarious existence. There was so much tyranny, so much fighting in the part of the country in which they lived, and after fighting usually came famine. In order to survive it was necessary for bygone ancestors of his to be continually on the alert. There was always the fear of being taken and tortured and killed by the enemy. The strain of being continually on the alert, of not even allowing oneself to sleep, however great the longing for it, produced in the race a capacity for disassociation, for a kind of dazed or half awake state, or an exhaustion through lack of sleep which, coupled with the fear, led on occasions to a temporary paralysis or to a detachment of the directing mind. Eventually more peaceful times came and they recovered some land. But the terrible times the family had been through left their mark upon the racial character

The fear of insecurity of life was deeply engraved on the subconscious mind of the race. There was also in the subconscious the characteristic of sleeping and yet being awake because of danger. We all know the dazed condition produced through not getting real sleep. It can cause a vacancy of mind, a semi-unconscious state when action is paralysed. The impressions would have faded from the racial mind in the peaceful times if it had not been that there was not always economic security. In bad days for the land there was for these people anxiety, a feeling of insecurity that kept alive the original racial fears.

This man would not have been affected by them if it had not been for a series of episodes in his life. When very young, so young he probably does not remember it, he was cuffed and knocked about the head and partially stunned.

Also his persecutor put him high up—I think on the branch of a tree from which he looked down and was terrified—feeling he would never get down. Later when he went up in a plane this ghost of a memory stirred, so his experience in a plane was harmful. But the experience of being half stunned so frightened the small boy he tried to forget it and did so by banishing the memory into his subconscious mind. This experience coupled with the racial inheritance formed a complex in the subconsciousness. It would have lain dormant and would never have harmed him if it had not been that when 15 or 16 he was kicked on the head. There came the dazed condition, the temporary vacancy of mind which was the racial habit or memory coming uppermost, dominating consciousness. Then there came the bad motor accident when he was as a young man rendered completely unconscious for some time. He recovered, for his brain was not in any way injured. But the experience greatly stimulated the complex; he was liable after that date to become its victim. If the old racial fear conditions were roused by alarm, or specially great anxiety and worry the unconscious condition, the dazed vacancy of mind were likely temporarily to appear, more particularly when he was driving a car which brought back the fear associations of the subconscious in connection with the accident, also the episode in his early boyhood.

It will be noted that he had the anxiety of driving a car not his own, and that he was especially worried and anxious about meeting his wife on the occasion of his black out when he drove into the ditch. If he had had no anxiety, if his mind had been serene the complex could not have controlled him and the episode would not have occurred.

He a is perfectly healthy normal man, and if he will realise that his unconsciousness and dazed condition when he was driving on this last occasion was due to events that had happened to his ancestors and later to himself in early life, and that they, therefore, belong to the dead past he need have no anxiety about himself in the future. He can drive a car with perfect safety. But there are two conditions attached to this. He should not drive a car if he is very anxious or worried. That might rouse the old racial fear and memories in the unconscious mind and lead to the production of a temporary vacancy of mind. Also he should not drive if he is extremely tired, for the racial inheritance, the old habit i.e. the dazed condition (half asleep half awake) might be reproduced and lead for a few moments or minutes to his losing control of the wheel. But I am quite satisfied that if he carries out these conditions and resolves the racial and personal complex by realising it as being a sham, dead, finished with, for it is of the past, there will be no recurrence of the "Black Out" and he can safely drive his car."

This account was read to the patient, the suggestions already made were reinforced and clarified. He resumed a normal active life, and has had no further trouble in driving or athletic activities for a matter of ten years. He has driven the same road since without accident.

This was a simple and straightforward case, but the addition of the sensitives full report and the convincing race history were of great assistance in the psychological treatment. His race history was known to some extent by himself and his family, and tallied in every respect with that recorded by the sensitive. His family had been driven into the West of Ireland, and had fought against wave after wave of savage invaders, and had faced famine and slaughter and persecution, through several centuries of the troubled history of that country. He accepted the story with the conviction of almost seeming personal knowledge.

The treatment enabled him to regain his confidence in himself completely.

It will be noted that no long investigation or psychoanalysis was employed to discover the basis of the complex. ESP supplied a quick and efficient substitute which was convincing to the patient, and served its purpose.

CASE XVII. CASE OF THE DOODLEBUGS

LADY B., (aged 60 years) came from the south coast of England, and consulted for continuous and incapacitating headache, of about a year's duration. This was seven years after the termination of the second world war. No treatment had been of benefit.

On physical examination except for four septic front teeth, no deviation from health could be discovered.

She had lived at the same house through the whole war, and unfortunately for her it was situated in the direct line of the doodlebugs on their journey to London. This entailed all the horrors of air-raid shelter life, and in addition, to the detonations of upwards of ten thousand A.A. guns, arranged in a ten mile circuit, with her home at the centre. (Incidently ninety-five per cent. of the doodlebugs were accounted for ultimately by these measures.) It must have been a noisy area. With her husband acting as an air-raid warden, and much older than herself, and a married daughter living in the same neighbourhood, Lady B's anxieties must have been intense. In the six or seven years after the war she was practically free from headaches, then they gradually supervened, and now were continuous. It was discovered on questioning that two or three aerodromes for jet-propelled aeroplanes had been established in the neighbourhood.

CASE XVII

It was suggested to her that a great deal of her trouble
was due to the noise of the jet-propelled aeroplanes
continually zooming overhead, which threw her mind back
into her terrible war years culminating in the doodlebugs.
The possibility of moving house to a quiet country place
was rejected as out of the question. Her anxiety about
her husband was pointed out to her. She made it clear
that it was her duty to go back. She was advised then on
her return to have her teeth removed, she was reassured
and given some medical treatment, and, with her
agreement, her psychological background was
investigated, by letter to England, with the subjoined
results:—

MAY 20th. 1953.

" Lady B., the writer of this letter, is a very well
balanced person. Hers is a strong character, an alert
mind with considerable practical ability and capacity for
organisation. She has an artistic feeling for perfection,
likes to have a well-kept house and her surroundings to
be harmonious. Hers is a subconscious craving for quiet,
for absence of jarring noise ; this craving derives from a
rooted complex of which she is unaware.

But she has no nerves or neurasthenia. Her headaches are absolutely real, not imaginary. But though
physical in character the headache she describes has a
fundamental non-physical origin. Its source is in the
unconscious mind of her race. Certain acute emotional
memories in this unconscious mind sowed the seed of an
anxiety complex in her subconsciousness. This complex
would have faded out if it had not been for certain alarming noise experiences that appear to have been hers when
she was an infant, or little more than an infant. These
helped the complex to develop.

When in later life she lived over a period of years in the midst of noise in perilous circumstances the complex became active. But so strong is her character and healthy her constitution it did not effect her physical health until recently when the noise of planes passing overhead evoked subconscious memories of the crash of bombs, the noise of shelling and shooting, the loud clamour of warfare which she had experienced in the second world-war.

There are various contributory factors in regard to these headaches from which she suffers. But the first cause in the racial memory springs from war conditions experienced by an ancestor of hers.

This ancestor was a soldier who had to fight unseen foes in wild solitary country. There was bush all round him. He had a position of responsibility as the officer in command. I get a feeling of hot sun and splitting headache caused by it. In spite of the noises and pain in his head he tried to carry on though he really should have delegated his authority to another. In fact he insisted on pushing on in spite of a subordinate advising against it.

But when his headache from the sun and its accompanying feeling of sickness was at its worst, he and his men were ambushed and a considerable number killed or badly wounded. The Sergeant, the subordinate was one of the dead. It was all a very sudden and shocking affair. Out of the stillness came the piercing whoops, other fear evoking sounds and the sharp cracking of rifles. These were intensified for the young officer by the noises in his head.

Afterwards he was not blamed for the ambush and the loss of life. In his report of the circumstances he never mentioned his confused judgment from headache at the time, and no one gave him away. The one who could have told was dead.

But the young officer had a conscientious sense of responsibility as regards his men's lives. The experience produced a morbid feeling of guilty fear in his mind. Tormented with headache, he had been too proud to relinquish authority, and in his opinion he was the murderer of these soldiers who took orders from him. Owing to his parents having been rather stern, dominating people imbued with calvanistic views on religion, they had imparted to him a morbid conscience easily made formidable by a feeling of guilty fear that might be roused by any error or transgression.

He never spoke to anyone of his guilty conscience in regard to the ambush. But the conflict it occasioned preyed upon his mind all his life and when he reached middle-age produced a repetition of the sunstroke headache and sickness. Descendants of his inherited his subconscious feeling of guilt, and when they were young were the more impressed because in those times he had his headaches they made him unbearably irritable, more than anything because of their psychological cause.

All this happened long ago and would not have affected Lady B. if it had not been for certain experiences of hers as a baby. A baby before it can think has a very sensitive subconsciousness that is easily impressed and frightened. The nurse or woman in charge of B. as a baby for a period, made loud sharp noises at her, and when the baby cried from fear the nurse slapped her instead of soothing and comforting her. This happened more than once and so increased her fear. The nurse was at all times talkative and excitable. A young baby needs quiet when it is as highly sensitive and highly bred as Lady B.

The conscious reasoning self has not started to develop in a small baby, so its subconscious mind was all the more easily impressed by a sense of insecurity and violence that corresponded in Lady B's later life to the violent and noisy war conditions in which she lived for years.

There are therefore three psychological causes for her headaches.

(1) The original guilty fear that was almost life-long in the soldier-ancestor with its physical expression in headaches, a weakness passed on to certain descendants—ancestors of Lady B.

(2) Her own marked fear experiences repressed by her into the subconsciousness when she was a baby, these forming a complex of anxiety.

(3) Her experiences in the last war. Being a very brave woman she suppressed then the natural fear of the noisy death-dealing doodlebugs and planes and guns. This fear suppressed below the level of conscious thought was much accentuated by the racial guilt conscience associated with war, shooting and death.

Thus in her case there was a cumulative repression and suppression of fear that formed a formidable anxiety complex in her subconscious mind, of which at the time she was unaware.

After the second world-war her physical condition was good ; and the relief of peace and change to a quiet less noisy country prevented any uprush from her subconscious complex producing headaches of the kind that had been induced in past generations of her family.

But in later years as an elderly woman she had much less resistance power from the physical aspect. For one thing there is some poison from three or four very bad teeth draining into her system. Secondly, she has recently been living at a place where the frequent noise of planes had roused the buried memories of fear and anxiety that form the complex in her subconscious mind. These create great tension that explains the tight feeling in her head. The mental tension is such it affects her physical nervous system, which is now more easily affected than formerly owing to her being an elderly woman.

First of all, therefore, she has to resolve this complex by reviewing the causes of the fears that create the physical tension, realsing that they belong to the dead past, are a fantasy without any foundation ; that there is nothing to fear from war, bombs or guns. She is no longer defenceless as she was when a baby in charge of an alarming noisy woman. Noise can no longer affect her, and the guilt fear from the racial memory which created an actual physical tendency to have headaches through tension is also of the dead past, so has no power over her.

A fact to realise is that one result of the complex is that her body is tense as she lies in bed before going to sleep. She must therefore practise relaxing every part of it, beginning first with her face and then gradually relaxing every muscle in her body. While doing so she might for a few moments visualise herself as waking up in the morning without a single ache in her head, without any ringing in her ears. Having previously resolved and abolished thereby her subconscious anxiety complex, that is the primary cause but not quite the whole cause of her headaches, she will fall into a natural sleep.

But the removal of these very bad teeth is necessary as they appear to be a factor in the case.

Also there seems to be near the base of the neck in the upper part of the spine some congestion. This may be the second contributory cause of the headaches, and manipulation, a few treatments by an osteopath would remove the congestion and also help to relieve the physical tension and pressure on the nerves of the head.

If she carries out these instructions and above all resolves the complex she will gradually free herself from these headaches which are primarily caused by the fear tensions in her subconscious mind.

All the same she should not neglect the two secondary causes, her teeth and the spinal congestion. The latter is not serious, but it possibly has a certain physical effect as regards the headaches."

When this account was submitted to Lady B. she was able to confirm that her ancestors had for very many years been soldiers in India, her husband had had a most distinguished career there during World War One. She had a detailed memory of the cruel nurse in her childhood; the discovery of this much impressed her. The treatment meted out to her by this cruelty had left an indelible scar on the child mind.

On her return home she carried out the treatment advised. She had the teeth removed, and visited an orthopaedic specialist. Two years later, she writes that the continuous headaches have disappeared, though occasional attacks of minor headaches recur. She considers that the treatment together with the knowledge of her psychological background were of very great help to her.

CASE XVIII. AN UNFINISHED CASE

IT is not reasonable to be asked or expected to deal with medical problems of healing by post. The human touch, the bond between doctor and patient, between the healer and the sick, is essential. If this is the case with physical ailments it is even more so with those that are psychological. It should be a rule not to undertake such cases or investigate their psychological background, by

ESP, except when treatment could be applied personally. The sensitive has always been advised that her province is perception by ESP, not actual therapy. Therapy is the work of the psychiatrist, not the sensitive.

In the following three cases this rule was not observed for particular reasons:—

The first wrote " . . . I am a doctor, I am desperately in need of help and should be eternally grateful, if such could be forthcoming." Coming from a professional colleague this request could hardly be refused. A summary of his complaints was sent and an article he had been in contact with, and from these an analysis of his case was obtained, by ESP, and sent to him.

This is the summary:—

"First I find it very difficult to describe that from which I suffer. It is a problem from the unconscious, which I have not been able to fathom.

Essentially I feel that there is something missing in my personality, so that I feel constantly incomplete, hence unable to mix on equal terms with people, a misfit, depressed and rather helpless. Life has been a constant struggle against I know not what.

I feel that I am constantly haunted or obsessed by I know not what, so that it interferes with my physical efforts, my interests, and my intellectual functioning.

I can get going best—that is I feel a sense of freedom —when working alongside another man, as if part of him. I feel lacking in resources when alone, while the presence of women— with the possible exception of prostitutes of whom I have little experience — flattens me out completely, and I feel nothing, dead. I feel like one who is half born, and that further development is denied, as if being murdered or perhaps just imprisoned and left to die. . .

My first insight into my disturbance was when I discovered a sexual interest in men, none in women—and it was only after considerable analysis that I began to realize how very much wider the problem was. I feel that nothing exists within me, that I have to obtain everything from outside, this being the basis of my sexual interest, for only in this way can I experience my sexual feelings. I have tried everything. I cannot alter, I can only repress, which I do considerably and it makes me ill.

Life for me has been one long struggle against unknown odds. I have forced myself to marriage and to parenthood. My medical work, at which I am considered rather above the average, I like when I am immersed in it, but it is an effort to get going. My real interests were architecture and music, especially conducting. This latter does give me a sense of freedom and achievement.

I have had years of psycho-analysis, and am now in the middle of the most helpful of all, a Jungian one, but I feel that the problem is deeper than the personal psyche, and I have never been able to bring the complex to the surface of my consciousness.

I would therefore be more than grateful for any help that can be given.''

In due course an ESP investigation was made, from an old tie that had been sent with the summary, and it was forwarded to the Doctor with some general advice from the writer.

ESP INVESTIGATION

"This man belongs to a highly civilised group. Oversensitive, with a quick perceptive mind, he is the psychological product of his racial past, of a tragedy that occurred many years ago of which he has no knowledge.

He may have been told that he is a victim of a mother complex. His own study of psychology would seem to have indicated to him that he is abnormal; it has suggested that in his nature there are certain factors of which he should be profoundly ashamed. This is an entirely wrong conclusion. He should feel no shame and he has brilliant gifts of which he should be proud. He is not in the true sense of the word abnormal. He is the victim of events that took place in the far past. Remove their drama from his life and he will find his normal self.

Many years ago ancestors of his lived in Flanders and also in north eastern France. They were weavers and made beautiful cloth which led to their developing artistic sensibilities. They were a fine race with a high code of morals and at that time deeply religious in the true sense of the word. There were four figures in the tragedy that controls their descendant's life. The first X, a man, the second Y—Yvonne, a woman, the third Z, a man, the fourth Religion, or that fine sensitivity, that subtle apprehension that is not to be confused with the church and mere piety, at least it was not so in X as a youth.

X, the son of a weaver and a Hugenot, was chosen in his boyhood to be the companion of the only son of a member of the nobility. It was considered a great honour that he should live at the chateau as if he were the foster brother of Z. The two boys became devoted to each other. Both Hugenots they shared all their thoughts and their experiences. It would seem that few brothers were such friends, so bound up in each other. Z had none of the fine sensitivity of X; he was innately coarse and cruel. But the boys were separated when their characters began to develop in adolescence. X went back to his home and worked as his father's apprentice. He met and married Yvonne, a beautiful girl whom he adored. Unfortunately when Z met Yvonne he developed a violent passion for her. As a result there was an estrangement between him and X.

When the persecution of the Hugenots began Z had no difficulty in changing his faith in order to preserve his possessions and his chateau. On learning of this, X became even more disillusioned as regards his one time friend. To make matters worse Z became a zealous fanatic, denouncing the Hugenots and causing even X's own family to be arrested, and they died for their faith. Thus Z was the murderer of X's father and brothers, but for X he reserved another fate. He had him conveyed to the chateau and imprisoned in a small cell in which he existed in continual darkness with rats as his only companions. Y was a timorous woman and largely through fear of torture she became a Catholic and Z made her his mistress. To satisfy his sadistic instincts Z had X occasionally taken out of his cell. Bound hand and foot and gagged he had to witness Z making love to his wife. He perceived that she responded. So there fell upon him the despair of complete disillusionment. Years passed, the wretched man still lived on. But release came at last when Z died suddenly. A servant in the chateau had remained a secret adherent of the Hugenots' faith and to him, in the confusion at the time of the death, X owed his freedom.

Y was turned out of the chateau a beggar by the cousin of Z who inherited it. She rejoined her husband and implored his forgiveness telling him that it was only through fear of torture and death she had surrendered herself to Z and changed her religion. It was not by any means the whole truth and X knew it. But he took his wife back and together they escaped to England. In his heart he never forgave her, and because of his underlying bitterness and his sternness and the fact that he had become a hideous old man through his past miseries, he became physically repulsive to her. His physical need led him to force himself upon her. She conceived a child, when she had a horror of sexual life with this man, and she carried that child through bitter months of despair knowing that life must continue for her while she was on earth. But she died in giving birth to the child. Thus was created the complex which controls her present living descendant. It was reinforced by the father's remorse at his wife's death. For he felt he was her murderer.

Various circumstances in the early life of the patient turned him in to his portion of racial experience.

But he must try to realise that he is haunted by what is dead and of the far past. If he fully realises this the obsession of these tragic experiences will vanish. Feeling will revive and his development continue. It was unfortunate that his natural bent for a purely creative life was denied him. If it had been possible for him to follow the profession of architect or musician it would have been far easier for him to escape from the prison of the past and realise his full nature. Not taking up either profession he developed a subconscious feeling of frustration that left him more open to the invasion of the past.

His forcing himself to marriage and to parenthood reproduced and therefore drew to him the experience of Y and X in that last unhappy year, and that increased the power of the complex. If before marriage he had known and fully realised the implications of this past history his marriage would have been a happy normal experience giving the necessary completion of his nature.

There is a minor factor to be noted in this case. He seems to have lived rather too much in the life of the mind and thereby put a heavy tax on his physical nervous system. If he could find an out-of-door occupation of physical energy and also of mental relaxation he would certainly benefit by it. The occupation need not be anything violent, but it should after a while produce a certain amount of physical fatigue that would help to rest the active brain and eventually give more vigour to the body.

There are other accessory facts in this case. When an infant this man was too severely punished for the special interest a baby often takes in the natural functions of the body. He was punished by a woman and terrified by her. It developed a fear he suppressed of women and a repressed dread of the sexual act. So only from outside has he been able to experience sexual feelings. But this event in infancy would not have had these reactions if it had not been for the racial experience already related. This man's infantile experience helped to link him up with the past tragedy.

Other events experienced by ancestors descending from X and Y strengthened by their attitude of mind the unconscious memory of that disaster. But it is sufficient to give the one clear cut experience and show its link with the punishment in early childhood.

This man works best alongside of another man partly because of the history of some of his male ancestors. As weavers they worked beside other men. But it was in the emotional life they were for generations much affected by men. X and descendants of his were religiously minded. His descendants became imbued with that stern type of faith that took its views from St. Paul who regarded sex as sinful, but held that it was "better to marry than to burn." So such men, though satisfying their physical desire with women, expressed their higher emotional life almost solely in religion. And they lived their faith fanatically only working for it with men. Intercourse with women was degraded in their minds. She had no share in those higher emotions, for she was suggestive of sin and evil. In modern times such religious belief lost its grip upon the minds of

X's descendants.   But it left its mark on the most sensitive
personalities in the race.

It will be seen therefore how formidable is the collective
experience in the far past of this man's family.   But he has
both courage and brilliance of mind.   He can perceive the
issues clearly, and knowing them now, he, if he exerts
himself, will overcome their harmful effects.   For they
belong to the past which is dead and finished with.   He will
break out of his racial prison, and then that unborn half is
born and he obtains completion of his nature.   It will
require great tenacity on his part and may take some time
because he has suffered so long from this complex.   But it
is absolutely possible for him to overcome it.   He might
use some auto suggestions, repeating them aloud for the
benefit of his subconscious mind just before he falls asleep.

"I am a living man in every sense of the word.   I am
through my gifts superior in many respects to the mass of
men.   I am able to express myself not only in work and
in art but in sexual life completely.   I am no longer
the victim of the false religious fears of my ancestors, nor
of the furtive infantile shame."

He might select from these and such like phrases, and
try their effect upon his subconscious mind when he is
getting drowsy just before sleep comes.

There is one physical difficulty in Dr. W's case which
retards his recovery.   He has tired out his physical nervous
system through too much introspection.   His mind first
preyed upon his body, overexcited his adrenal glands,
making them excessively active and overworked the actual
physical nerves.   Now, these through the past drain on
them, prey upon his mind, are factors in keeping him
depressed and despondent.   A mental reorientation would
improve his physical condition and also help him a long
way towards recovery.

He should try, even for a short time daily, to practice the mental discipline and bodily exercise I shall later suggest.

He must bear in mind that we are ruled by our habits and our inheritance from the race-mind to a very great extent.

Dr. W has over far too long a period been wedded to the one habit, too much concentration on the conflict in his ego. The conflict—to put it crudely—is due to his having had too many ancestors of a pronounced religious temperament with, at the same time, strong sexual instincts. These two were continually at war. The religious sense and religious fears protesting that these instincts were sinful and had to be repressed, and when they were expressed it was a lowering and shameful thing. This racial sense of guilt and attempts at repression in part account for the numbed feeling and lack of energy, distaste for women in their descendant, W.

But W has lost the anchor of his ancestors, which steadied them, and that anchor was a profound and emotional belief in God or the Divine Mind which harmonized all things. W has none of this real belief in an Unknown Power. Many men do not need to have a belief in God. But this man W, because of his racial history, urgently needs its modern equivalent. He has, for the sake of his mental health, to escape from his ego as his ancestors did by sensing the Divine Mind, and seeking to forget himself even for a brief time each day, by making himself one with it.

This can be done in that regular time allotted daily.

(1) By his abandoning this painfully cruel concentration on his own ego.

(2) By relaxing his body and stilling his mind.

(3) Then he should cast his thoughts outwards, compel himself to reflect on some expression of the Divine Mind. The stars or the Galactic System, or the workings of nature on earth, some part of the mighty creation of the Universe. He should then imagine himself as being a part of it. He should thus, during this exercise, banish the idea that he is merely a disintergrating psychic atom, mentally completely isolated from the rest of the universe, cut off, impotent. He must try to regard himself as a part of that ever creating life which I call the Divine Mind. He should recognise his own littleness in that vast ever creating impulse and his greatness in the power he has to create.

By the practice in silence and quiet of such contemplation of the Divine mind and its mystery he will in time become detached from himself and thus give his tortured self rest and the chance to recuperate. Gradually through such exercises of the mind he becomes one with the creative life and heals himself. Physician heal thyself. This can be done through detaching his mind from himself and contemplating the functioning of nature and the universe and allowing the healing stream of the Life Force or Divine Force to flow into him through his reflection on them and connection with them each day for a time.

It would be helpful to him if he went and dug in a garden, watched the growth of life from seed to plant, plant to flower, puzzled over it, sought for the secret of its growth. He should fill his mind with the observations of every detail of that harmonious spontaneous growth. It would be an object lesson—that he is not to force or compel himself to creative acts. They should come easily, spontaneously, as they do in nature. If he had time to go for a walk alone in country or forest he should again try to

K

throw his mind outwards, study even the leaves of the trees, their development from a bud, the changing colours as the season passes, their texture and form.

The Universe is the Life Force's thinking, its mind. To look, therefore, into the deeps of the Firmament or at Nature is to look into the Divine Mind. From looking comes, if one lets oneself go, a gradual identification with it, a unification of W's broken and tortured self. And from that reconciliation can come for him a fresh mind, greatly increased energy and creative impulse.

Dig in the garden, study the process of growth in a garden. Walk in the country, study skies, trees and field. By losing his own little personal thoughts through thoughts of the mystery behind the creation of these things he saves his mind and escapes from wretchedness and despair. It will take time and great effort at first. But the physician has it in his power to heal himself on these lines and also by following his Jungian analyst's advice, as the latter is getting at the root of his trouble. But once all has been unearthed the cure would seem largely to be in the practice of identification with the larger self of Nature and the universe, wherein there is the harmony of pulsating creative imagination and its full glorious expression."

The Doctor replied:—

". . . I was rather taken aback and stunned by the information contained in the report. I do not feel better, in fact I feel much worse, whether on this account, I cannot say. *It certainly was rather a shock as it does in a way express something of what I feel.* I feel numbed and without life, haunted by an unknown something that I cannot place."

I wrote on two further occasions, the doctor replied that he had not improved. He had submitted the ESP script to the Jungian analyst, who he stated suggested *that it might be his myth, and he thought he might be able to use it.* In one further letter he was overwhelmed by the disastrous consequences of the N.H.S. on his practice, it is to be regretted that it was impossible to follow up the case.

It was clear from the failure in this case that it is unwise to attempt to deal with a case of this nature of evident long standing, without any personal interviews, moreover the evidence obtained does not appear to have been utilized in a firm manner by the Jungian analyst. He created doubt when he suggested it *might* be his myth, instead of employing the encouraging aspects of the report.

It is suggested that the patient had become what might be termed " a psycho-Analysis addict," long prior to the ESP investigation. His case should not have been attempted.

CASES XIX AND XX. THE AUSTRALIAN CASES.

AGAIN the inadvisability of interfering at a distance was considered. But the urgency and the pathetic nature of the first case and the fact that every possible measure had been attempted, including both psychiatric and spiritual help, led to an ESP investigation being undertaken. The husband of the patient wrote a letter that indicated the serious nature of his wife's illness, and the quality of the help which was sought.

Mr. X's letter:—

Dear Dr. Connell,
. . . My wife and I have been married for nine years.
. . . About 2½ years ago, a despondency and restlessness *and a desire to die entered into my wife.* She said, " It does not make sense, for I have everything I want." . . .
Later deep-seated cancer was discovered and thought to be the cause. It was successfully removed. There was six

months of happiness and *then the desire to die returned.*
It appeared to be without cause, no recurrence of the cancer
was observed. The best surgical and medical men, a psycho-
analyst, and a spirit healer, were all baffled. The cause
of the depression appeared to be beyond their reach . . .
This hidden pull had operated in her father's case also. He
committed suicide. I am certain that in both cases there
is a hidden factor more powerful than themselves. Could
you help us ? . . .

Signed X

This briefly expresses the problem I was asked to
consider. I told Miss Cummins that in my opinion the
recurrence of the cancer appeared inevitable from the
extensive nature of the operation. I obtained her report
and sent it with a letter of advice on its use.

Analysis by Geraldine Cummins

August 14, 1949.

" The patient, Mrs. C., is sensitive, highly intelligent
and is not neurotic; but she is the victim of an invasion,
an invasion by events that occurred generations back in
her family history. This memory resides in the unconscious mind of her race. It is as follows:—

Many years ago,—in Georgian times—ancestors of
hers lived in England. There were two brothers who
were greatly attached to each other. I will call them
John and Thomas. Thomas was serious-minded and
interested in religion. John was gay and lived in the
passing moment. Unfortunately, both brothers fell in
love with the same girl, Mary. When Thomas learned of
John's love he had scruples about competing with him
and kept away from the girl. So John married Mary.
Then seeing Mary as the happy wife of his brother, Thomas
became jealous and resentful. But his religious nature
led him bravely to suppress his passion for her. He went
away and became a preacher and belonged to some
religious sect, in fact made it his absorbing life's work.

John was an agricultural labourer. He had several children by his wife Mary. But he was very badly paid, and at least two of the children, who were undernourished, died. They died of this dire poverty. One survived.

Mary was beautiful. John's employer made advances to her, promised her husband a better wage if she would be his mistress. When she resisted he became threatening. He would dismiss her husband from his employment and evict them from their cottage. Times were bad. This dismissal would mean starvation or separation of husband, wife and child in the workhouse, which then was a horrible place.

At this time, Thomas, who thought he had conquered his love for his brother's wife, returned to that locality and visited John. John had just learned of his employer's infamous offer to his wife. He had found it out by eavesdropping. For the sake of her child and husband's future Mary had consented to go secretly to the employer's house at night if the latter would send John away for periods on business or work of some kind. The two brothers raged together about it, and finally, John went that evening to visit his employer. He had a furious scene with him and was thrown out of this man's house and dismissed from his employment.

Though he did not realise it at the time, Thomas's passion for Mary was reawakened. He broke into Y, the employer's, house that night. He did not go with intent to kill. He was simply blind with rage. But Y, surprised in his bedroom, attacked Thomas with a weapon. In the struggle for it Thomas killed him, then escaped by the bedroom window. John was arrested and tried for this. Various suspicious circumstances made it seem to Judge and jury quite certain that he had murdered his employer. He was sentenced to death.

During the trial Thomas had decided that if the sentence on his brother was death he would confess to the killing and give himself up. But when the time came to do so his passionate love for Mary was such he said nothing and let his brother be hanged for the homicide he had committed. It was not murder, for it was accidental, done in self-defence. The murder he committed was that of his brother by—through his love for his wife—letting him die for his offence.

Shame and starvation seemed the only prospects before Mary as she desperately told Thomas after the hanging of her husband. Thomas argued to himself he could only save her from that by marrying her. To escape from the terrible memories of his brother's end he accepted a job as missionary in Australia. The two, therefore, got married and went out there.

But Thomas could not escape from memory in another country. He had loved his brother, and was soon—once his passion for Mary was satisfied—suffering in a hell of remorse. It became unendurable. He felt he had no right to Mary and ought therefore to kill himself. But he could not, he argued, leave her without a man to work for her—leave her in dire poverty in a strange land.

Mary noticed his deep melancholy. She probed for the reason, and because of his need to share his guilt and through her clever probing he confessed, told her the whole story and the problem of his guilt. She had just conceived a child by him. In the months she carried the baby she brooded over this tragedy and tortured herself with the idea that she was to blame; that she had tempted Thomas.

The birth of their child was difficult. It was a large baby. Actually there had to be some kind of operation for the baby to be born. After the birth when Mary had physically recovered, she and Thomas did not live any longer as husband and wife. But mentally they lived together, in their daily companionship they shared the same guilty secret. It was like a cancer tumour in their minds, poisoning their life together. At last Thomas thought he could overcome it by living with her, by forcing himself on her against her wishes one night. This was the final blow, as it seemed she thus committed a crime —the crime of living with her husband's murderer. So she committed suicide though she loved life. It was a wrong act, for thus she deserted her little boy, left him to a father half mad from remorse.

Now the influence during the pre-natal period of her thoughts about the transgression of having a child by her husband's murderer all formed a racial complex and also built it up in the mind-body of the baby. Later on the widowed father's melancholy influence and thoughts about the tragedy affected the child's sub-conscious mind, increased the harm already done. In his mental-body that boy through life carried the cancer-tumour of the crime which expressed itself in physical cancer in his adult life. The boy was not Mrs. X's father. I think another generation or more intervened.

But Mrs. X's father was highly sensitive and therefore susceptible over the years to the cancer tumour of crime carried in the unconscious memory. He finally expressed it physically in his material body. But the operation did not remove it from his mental-body, and there was again repeated in his mental-body Mary's agonising problem. There had been for her ' the deep pull back to death.' It seemed to her that her only right course was to kill herself and thus rejoin her wronged murdered husband. She could not continue to live with his murderer. But she did wrong in deserting her child by committing suicide. This act was repeated by the patient's father under the driving influence of the ancestral memory of Mary's life and suicide and the remorse of Thomas, all lying in the unconscious mind.

In these past years of adult life Mrs. X has been faced with the same situation, and like her father, experiences mentally *the deep pull back to death.* But if she yields to it she will commit again the crime of murder, the unforgivable transgression. She deserts not only her child but a husband who is the reincarnation of John. Is John to be betrayed a second time? It is in a different manner, but it is a similar betrayal to the one in the past. Here is the question she only can answer.

Mrs. X. has to realise that the transgression was the murder of his brother by Thomas through his letting him be hanged for his own crime. The matter she mentions that was used in the mind-body of the transgressor, was passed on through the generations. It was in the mind-body of Mrs. X.'s father. From him she inherited it. His life, his suicide all impressed her subconscious mind, strengthening its connection with the Tragedy.

You will remember that in giving birth to the child Mary had to have an operation. When Mrs. X. was faced with an operation for cancer the mental emotional impression of it helped to link her up with the Mary episode and with her tragic suicide, led it to get a grip of her subconscious mind. Hence its influence over the consciousness of a woman much later in time producing as Mrs. X., calls it *the deep pull back to death* after her recovery from the operation.

After her ancestor Mary recovered physically, she was faced with the problem of living with Thomas or by her death going to comfort and be with her first husband John. liable to give way to the *pull of death* though John in the descendant has allowed herself to be caught in that ancestral emotional experience. She is giving way or is liable to give way to the *pull of death* though John in the person of her husband is alive and with her. Merely even to allow this emotional ancestral memory to govern her moods is bringing the shadow of death into the lives of her husband who was and remains John and into her son's life. She has to recognise the deception, she has to realise that there is only one way to expiate the original transgression, one way to destroy the sense of guilt in the mind-body and that is by life, by more living in every sense of the word for her husband and her son, by a supreme effort banishing all thought of death from her consciousness, making up her mind to live, live as long as is possible for the sake of her husband, for the sake of the John of long ago. Thus is the power of the racial tragedy broken, and it will never again be repeated.

This is the treatment she has to follow. She must seek to live fully, be much out of doors when possible. She has to form a habit of thinking, of living for her husband and son. Thus is expiation made for John's life cut-off so early in a previous generation."

Letter from the Husband, Mr. X
Dear Dr.,

. . . The story unfolded by Miss Cummins is both unusual and convincing. My wife became deeply impressed in each successive reading, of the truth of the story . . . It might be said by a critic, "Miss Cummins successfully sensed our problems and clothed them in a dramatic narrative. She cannot prove the truth of the story." Fortunately, however, we can go deeper than this, for the literal truth of the story stands or falls on the statement that *Thomas came to Australia three to five generations ago.* I am sure I gave you no clue in my letter to show whether my wife was from England or from an old established Australian family. I could not have given you this, because I thought her father came from South Africa myself. I have since learnt as a fact that he was born in an obscure town in New South Wales (incidentally, Thomas, in going to Australia, sentenced himself to transportation to what was then the penal settlement of the Empire).

My wife's father was dominated by some Nemesis which dogged his life with depressive moods, and he finally committed suicide. His father, from hearsay, suffered from fits of passion and depression . . .

Unfortunately, as was reported later, the cancer recurred and Mr. X's wife was given only two months to live—but he continues:

The conviction of the truth of the narrative has relieved the tension in my wife's mind and has completely banished the desire to die.

Later Mr. X reported:

My wife died, and yet in a curious way I am convinced that, though she lost the physical battle, she won the real one. From the time my wife received Miss Cummin's manuscript an inner tension eased and vanished. There was no longer a sense of struggling and frustration, but a calm acceptance of her lot, and a deeper spiritual understanding. She radiated happiness. When at her request she was told that the cancer had returned, she simply said, " I will not be a wet blanket. I will make the very best of what is left." In a little while she was laughing and making jokes with the doctors. In the last weeks her unforced cheerfulness and tranquility amazed everyone. She inspired all who came to cheer her, by her courage.

In dying, she inspired the living. No person is truly dead who lives in the minds of others. Doctor, I must thank you and Miss Cummins for your real help.

In a later letter Mr. X. writes:— "Though Miss Cummins's manuscript came too late to save my wife, yet it was responsible for those last two months when she was free from pain and marvellously poised and serene in her mind . . .

I think that the ancestral lines of John and Mary met once again in my wife and myself. Again many thanks."

Case XX. The 2nd Australian Case

Four years later I was again asked by Mr. X. to assist in the same manner in the case of a friend of his. Again in this case it was stated that the best medical and psychological advice had already been obtained, with great benefit, but leaving a residuum of terror that made life extremely difficult for the victim.

Briefly the patient's own letter stated : —

. . . My age 47 years. At 18 years suddenly (after working for some weeks with a gang of very rough labourers) I found myself quite incapable of urinating, in the company of others, with an accompanying fear thought " *What will they think if they know* ? "

Since then I can seldom go for more than an hour, less sometimes, without needing to urinate . . .

You can imagine the subterfuges I have been driven to . . .

. . . During the last war I went to pieces for a time— from this fear . . .

. . . There are times when I have the idea of being possessed by an evil spirit . . .

. . . Sometimes I have thought I was malingering . . .

. . . It is like being in a dark room with something evil that is about to hurt you terribly . . .

. . . My father had the same difficulty but not consciously.

I have been told that my mother suffered much at my birth. The fear " *What would they think if they knew* ? " drove my mother to bouts of drinking . . .

In my case three treatments of " truth drug injections " during which suggestions that the trouble would come to the surface were made, and they have proved ineffectual.

Could you help me ?

(Signed) K.C.

155

We have here a psychological problem of twenty-nine years persistance, expressed *physically* as an embarrassing urge to micturate and an inhibition, expressed *psychologically* as an unknown causeless fear, only slightly benefited by expert psychiatric treatment.

I sent the analysis I obtained from Miss Cummins, with a letter of advice on its use.

I emphasised to Mr. X. that the story must be utilized with firm confidence, to be beneficial. It must not be referred to with doubt as " possibly his racial myth " as was done in the case of the disappointed doctor.

Miss Cummins's Analysis (somewhat condensed)

"The writer of this letter is a sane, normal and a fine type of man. He is not neurotic; in the sense that the term is ordinarily used.

My impression is that he is the innocent victim of terrible experiences of certain ancestors of his. I think that the psycho-analyst, and K's friends discovered all but the root cause of his trouble, the fundamental cause. His mother's experiences at the time of his birth, certain unfortunate experiences he has himself related in his letter, other matters the psycho-analyst succeeded in uncovering, might be described as contributory causes, or rather, they were unfortunate occurrences in that they laid him open and receptive to two tragedies that took place, (1) in the far past of his race and (2) in the nearer past. If his birth, the early sheltered life and the unfortunate experience he had at the age of 18 years had not been to a certain degree in *the pattern and of the vibratory quality* of his ancestors' tragedy he would have led an ordinary happy life unhaunted by any fear. The very phrase *What will they think if they know* was the uttered and muttered thought of ancestors who participated in two tragedies. These racial

156

memories lay in his unconscious mind and came into intense and harmful life and were activated (1) by his mother's experience and fear at his birth, (2) the experiences in childhood of a too sheltered existence and (3) the reaction to the tough men at the age of eighteen.

The ancestral tragedies are rather a long story. I will be brief. Each tragedy is in the same emotional pattern, the keynote in each case being *What will they think if they know?*

Tragedy One

The following occurrences took place in a northern island — Scotland, it seems. The two whose record has influenced K were a young man and woman I shall call Donald and Sheila. Sheila was the daughter of a Chief C. An uncle of Donald, M was the Chief of a rival clan. C. was more powerful, and also he was very patriotic and hated the English. Sheila and Doald became attracted, met, and were married secretly.

M, the uncle of Donald, was intriguing with the English. Before there was open war Donald met Sheila and urged her to fly to England, he was so apprehensive of their future. She was not prepared for this and refused to go with him then. In any case a signal of danger was given, and she and her escort hurried away. To cut a long story short her father's stronghold was soon besieged by an English force and their ally M and his clan. M knew of the attachment between Sheila and Donald. She was the victim. She was led to believe by Donald that he and some of his clan were secretly on her father's side and wanted to enter the castle in order to defend it for her father C. So, one dark night, she opened the gate of the castle to them. The besieging force had that day made a feint of withdrawing from the siege. In consequence the defenders of the castle were not on the alert and were easily overcome once the raiders had rushed in through the opened gate.

That mob of rough clansmen and soldiers as they crowded past Sheila, as gradually she realised *the treachery,* left an ineffaceable impression on the racial memory. They easily captured the stronghold by thus taking its defenders by surprise. *Then the unspeakable horror, the disillusionment of this* ancestress of K— drove her temporarily crazy. But it must be remembered that Donald was under sentence of death if he did not obey orders and carry through his plan.

When Sheila recovered her reason she found herself imprisoned with her father, mother and brother in a dungeon. They were being held as hostages. Sheila's mother died soon after their imprisonment began. Then Sheila discovered that she was carrying Donald's child. *Living those months in the dusk and darkness of that squalid confined dungeon with the father and brother she loved, the distracted woman's continual thought was 'What would they think if they knew?'* She was living in horrible conditions with the two to whom she was devoted and had unwittingly betrayed.

At times she was seized with moods of veritable panic when she cried and screamed. *Deep and terrible emotions are heavily cut and are like scars on the racial memory.* Thus the haunting of Kenneth (the patient) was initiated.

(1) *'What will they think if they know?'*

(2) Panic at being in an enclosed space with others.

(3) The overwhelming horror when these rough soldiers swarmed past Sheila through the opened gate of the stronghold and she realised that she had betrayed her own people and those she loved.

This ghostly memory connected up from K's unconscious mind with the tough men when he had that eighteen-year-old experience. *That is the original cause,* which was strengthened by further tragical experiences. A number of other factors contributed to the building up of K's complex. *But this was the primary one.* It would have faded from the unconscious or at least not had the same significance if it had not been that Tragedy Two in a later generation was emotionally in a similar pattern in many respects ; *so was like fuel feeding a sinking fire,* rekindling it in the racial unconscious mind.

Now, I will briefly tell of the further events in Sheila's history that relate to this pattern. She was removed from the dungeon to a fairly comfortable room shortly before hers and Donald's child was born. Eventually her father and brother were executed and she was compelled to witness their death. Then she was released and put in her husband's charge.

In the south, beyond the borders, Donald was granted an estate as a reward for his services. He loved Sheila, and her baby was his heir. But his life with her led him eventually to wish that he had refused to obey orders and had sacrificed his life, then in the prime of his manhood. For because of her *shattering experience, Sheila was to him mentally a desolation.* Much of the actual memories of her experience were repressed into her subconsciousness, because they were unbearable. She became frequently obsessed by the idea, for instance, that she was *in the grip of an evil spirit, mercilessly cruel and pitiless, that was forcing her to commit a dreadful and shameful act.* This was the expression of the complex of repressed memories. She had in this respect a very bad influence on her sensitive small son. *So when he grew up and she was dead,* he began to repeat the impression she had made on him at his most impressionable age. At times he was haunted by the belief that he was *in the grip of an evil spirit mercilessly cruel and pitiless that was forcing him to be a coward and a shameful character.* He had inherited a horror of fighting and war from his mother, and his father wished him to take up the honourable profession of arms. But he remained a coward, disgracing himself in that respect because in fact he could not help it, and he was despised for it by his father and his family.

Thus K's very sensitive self, mechanically at times registers a racial memory, is impelled by it when he becomes impressed by the idea of his being in the grip of an evil spirit. *But this mood would not have reached him, would have lost power if it had not been greatly reinforced by experiences emotionally similar that were experienced by a descendant of his, generations later in time.*

Tragedy Two

Though the writer of the letter has a fine tolerant mind and no church or narrow dogma appears to affect his wide charitable outlook, nevertheless he is through the unconscious *deeply affected* by a fantastically bigoted ancestor's life—a minister. We will call this ancestor John. He was descended from Donald and Sheila. But such had been the lapse of time and the changing fortunes of their descendants he was not aware of their history. *'What will they think if they know?'* had characteristically produced extreme reserve, and stories of the family were not passed on from generation to generation.

There was also a habit of melancholy introspection, an inherited inner fear bred from Tragedy One, that drove John into the study of religion. He became a believer literally in the everlasting fires of hell for the sinner and, above all, a believer in the power of the Devil ever ready to tempt the weak man. *He overcame melancholy by an assertion of religious superiority.* An eloquent preacher who led a model *and austere life, he became intensely superior and arrogant* as one of the few chosen by the Lord to be saved. He married a good but very unattractive and ugly woman. In temperament a *poet who loved beauty,* he harshly suppressed all that side of his nature. But what is suppressed occasionally takes its revenge. The stage was set and then he met Mary, a lovely young girl, who came of a bad-living family, was taking to bad ways herself. But she appeared to be rescued from them by the preacher John's eloquence. *She was sexually very attracted to the tall handsome minister and was really an unscrupulous jade.* She used to meet the minister as if by accident and then seek his advice about her father's bad ways. Gradually she roused the suppressed side of John's nature, his feeling for beauty. Without realising it, he became infatuated with her looks. Starved sexually, *he was unable to resist uncontrollable impulses.* But he was immediately filled with horror of himself and wild panic when he learned from her that she was with child, his child. *He had only twice with her fallen from grace,* as he called it, and did not, because of his innocence, even suspect the truth, that hers was another man's child. So when her father spoke to him with a sham fury, he accepted the paternity, and from that day was blackmailed for money. After a while he got into debt. Then the father became threatening and menacing.

Now John's congregation adored him as a saint, and he had an almost narcissus worship of himself, and lived for their admiration of his pious, austere character. *'What will they think if they know?'* was the phrase that haunted him day and night. Mary's father became a member of his congregation, and *Sunday after Sunday his menacing presence put the minister through the most excruciating*

L

torture. For the unfortunate man, preaching his sermon became a veritable hell because of his fear that at any moment he would be denounced before his congregation by his blackmailer.

Soon at services he conducted on Sunday *John nearly went mad from claustrophobia,* and the craving to escape from that crowd and that confined space. There came a time when he could bear it no longer and, with his wife and children, fled the district secretly by night, leaving his house and furniture to his creditors. He and his family then suffered great hardships owing to his having to remain in hiding for some time. Through sheer starvation *one of his children died.* He felt then that *he was its murderer.* Through his sin's consequence his son had died.

Following this death there came to him what I call the repetitive pattern of emotion. Haunted by the thought of the blackmailer, John developed the idea that he was *in the grip of an evil spirit, merciless and cruel.* It seemed that there was no hope for him and his dependants. But a local clergyman saved him on this occasion from complete collapse. He got parishioners to help and John and his family were rescued from dire poverty. John was given a job as a teacher. But he did not dare disclose his past even to this kind clergyman.

Unfortunately he remained a tortured victim though material circumstances were now all right for him and his family. For instance, *he felt guilty because he dared not send money for Mary's child* for fear of his being traced by her blackmailing father. Therefore he regarded himself as *a coward, a sham.* Gradually Mary's father filled his consciousness in a disguised form—the form of a demon, mercilessly cruel, who had made John a coward and a sham, one who was a cheat in that he had cheated the God he worshipped, cheated his children, his wife. All those about him looked on him as a good and model character, whereas he knew himself to be utterly evil in having ruined a young girl and left her to support her child. Such were his ruminations. I must pass over many details in this man's life. But because he had been an eloquent Bible preacher, 'one of the chosen of the Lord' in his opinion, he suffered in a way very few men would have suffered in such circumstances. He could not bear to be thought other than a fine and even noble character. So he could not face the publicity of his shame.

Then Mary's father rediscovered him, and again he was compelled to fly. From that time on he never stayed long in one place, and the shock of that second discovery persisted, making him more and more a hunted, haunted man, haunted by the phrase—'*What will they think*' etc. or by *the Evil Spirit and its increasing grip*.

The Reactions of the Patient K

(1) He had a fear-saturated ante-natal period. If there is sharp emotional experience the subconscious of the mother mingles with that of the baby shortly before birth and during birth, for emotion has a peculiar driving force. It was extremely harmful to K—. The deep dark condition of fear that impregnated his subconsciousness then made him susceptible to the racial double tragedy of fear-haunted lives, opened a closed door to it. (2) A sheltered childhood, (3) abrupt change to his experience with the tough men, inevitably produced the emotional pattern of the double tragedy.

(4) The war experiences. The two tragedies were the fundamental cause of K— going to pieces. In the first was the experience of Sheila when the rough soldiers, through her opening the gates, swarmed into her father's

stronghold, bringing war and fighting, and she knew the horror of having unwittingly betrayed those she loved.

When each Sunday the preacher faced the prospect of being denounced by his blackmailer during the service there was the repetitive emotion—a kind of unreasoning terror that on disclosure he would be attacked and lynched by the pious, calvinistically minded men of his congregation. K— has been, mirror-like, reflecting this concentrated racial fear at various periods in his life."

This is the story that I sent to my patient. In its original form it was more comprehensive. Exigencies of space led to its curtailment.

I advised him as fully as I could. Somewhat beyond my expectations, I received most grateful thanks by return of post.

Quotations from Mr. C.'s grateful letter are as follows:—

Dear Friends,

Please pardon my presumption but this seems the only correct form of address . . .

Your letter caused a real emotional upheaval—not yet subsided . . .

My unconscious accepted the story absolutely. It explained many things . . .

. . . But Doctor, incredible almost to me, my periods of needing to urinate have gone from the usual hour to 4 hours, never less than 3 ! I still find myself wondering if it is too good to be true . . .

. . . I saw the death of a demon, of the demon that had obsessed me . . .

Thanks were repeated many times, and the letter terminated :

. . . I find it so difficult to express my gratitude that I will not try.

Yours sincerely,

K.C.

About six months later two further letters of thanks were received and two beautifully turned pieces of woodwork, turned by Mr. C. himself from rare Australian woods.

Three years later he has remained cured.

As a physician I am concerned more with the curing of the sufferer than with the method employed. A certain drug will cure a certain disease—am I to withold it because I do not know how it acts?

In these cases a certain 'mental *tour de force*' of a remarkable nature has been performed by Miss Cummins. On her own admission she has no particular psychological knowledge or training.

Why and how does she succeed in producing two such uniquely opposite stories to cover and explain two such diverse psychological ailments? They are not the product of her conscious mind. (She is cultured; her father and grandfather were eminent physicians.)

What then is this subconscious mind that appears to travel with such facility some thousands of miles to Australia, and some hundreds of years back into English and Scottish lost history? Or was it true history? The writer has no proof but why are the stories accepted at once and without question by the patients? Is it because the memories were long buried in unknown recesses in the victims' unconscious minds and are recognized, like old forgotten friends? As a physician I can only utilize the information and record the facts in both cases as they have occurred, both patients were cured psychologically, the second in addition, of a physical disability.

Both had had previous psychiatric treatment including "truth drug" injection and treatment of a psychoanalytic nature before research by ESP was initiated.

CHAPTER III

PSYCHOMETRY OR OBJECT READINGS: AN ADVANCE ASPECT OF ESP

> . . . it appears to be a key phenomenon which when more fully understood will throw much light on the mysterious territory ranging between mind and matter.—
>
> *Raynor C. Johnson.*

WE have not further discussed the subject of the proof of ESP, which it has been shown in Chapter I has been amply established in the opinion of those scientists who have studied it.

We have now to proceed to consider the series of cases just recorded, which carry the question a shade further. These cases represent what may be termed applied ESP. They demonstrate how an adept in the exercise of ESP utilizes her developed faculty to advantage. It has also been demonstrated in these cases that ESP can be of signal help in the construction of the diagnosis of certain obscure psychoses—in some of which other methods of investigation in the hands of specialists had not succeeded, though in certain instances they had been of benefit. To succeed in tracking the primary cause or causes in these obscure cases by the usual psychological procedures might require six months or a year of fairly continuous treatment and analysis (e.g. Cases I, XII, XIX and XX).

It is submitted that it could have been of great help to an expert psycho-analyst in such circumstances to send let us say a specimen of the patient's handwriting, a fountain pen or some small object that had been used by the patient, to an expert psychometrist, or sensitive, asking for a report on the psychological background of the owner. This would correspond to the action of a physician when he sends a morbid specimen to a laboratory for a pathological or bacteriological report to assist him in the diagnosis and treatment of an obscure physical ailment. We note in passing that in such circumstances, the psychometrist or sensitive requires the same confidence and similar ancillary information of the clinical aspects of the case as the pathologist. Further, the specimen must be selected and despatched with the same or greater care if the result is not to be vitiated.

For all these reasons it is necessary to possess as complete a knowledge as possible of the ESP process if we wish to utilize it, and to co-operate adequately with an adept in applying this faculty to the best advantage.

Certain terms should first be defined: —

An adept is known under several names, as psychometrist, medium, percipient or "sensitive;" we have utilized the latter term.

In her investigation a sensitive may be asked to examine an object that has been closely associated with an individual.

The object is sometimes called "The directive," and as shall be seen the term is an expressive and convenient one.

The individual, who may be under investigation, is referred to as the "subject" (he may be alive or dead, known or unknown). In his book *The Imprisoned Splendour* (referred to at the commencement of this chapter) Raynor C. Johnson states that the most striking contributions to the subject of advanced ESP were those made by Dr. Eugene Osty while director of the Institute

Metaphysique International, in Paris. He made investigations with a number of talented French sensitives (both with and without hypnosis) over many years. His book was translated in 1923 by Stanley De Brath. Also he refers to Dr. J. Hettinger who confirmed much of Dr. Osty's work and performed much pioneer experimental work in addition.

The conclusions he has quoted, together with those brought to light in some of the cases recorded, and from a number of other sources, are submitted.

The Directive

(1) If an object is to be taken as a directive, it should be handled to the minimum degree possible, and if from a living subject, he himself, if present, should cover it with some smooth unused material — glazed paper or artificial silk for example, and suitably parcelled, send it to the sensitive.

(2) Any notes from the physician or investigator should be despatched under a separate cover—and in the case of a physician, he should give every relevant detail in the history of the illness that might be of help to the sensitive in exercising her special faculty, in elucidating the hidden psychological causes suspected of lying at the root of the psychosis.

It should here be emphasized that the sensitive must not be treated as if she were on her defence, and difficulties be deliberately, or carelessly put in the way of her research. The care in collecting and despatching the directive from the patient to the sensitive for example, is simply to prevent the directive from being overlaid, and saturated with the psychic impress of other individuals (somewhat as a contaminating organism carelessly introduced would vitiate a bacteriologist's report). The short note at the end of Case XIV illustrates the consequence of such carelessness, it vitiated the result that was anticipated. Again, when a physician wishes to investigate a psychological case, to send a sealed envelope containing a mysterious message is not the way to approach a sensitive, — it could be rendered quite useless for such a purpose if it had been carried by a messenger to a football match before delivery. It could have become overlaid with his excited emotional impress and the sensitive might be condemned as incompetent or a fraud because she described the more emotional football crowds—etc.

If in an analogous physical condition an X-ray picture of a patient's chest is required—it would be of tremendous help to the radiologist in making his report on the films he had taken, if he had been given the clinical and family history of tuberculosis, if any, before he formed his opinion.

The same applies to the sensitive. Her work should be facilitated by providing her with all relevant information to assist her in exercising her ESP faculties to the fullest advantage in tracing the psychosis to its source.

(3) In all psychometric investigations it should be realized that the directive is merely a point of connection between two living minds—or a connection between one living mind (that of the sensitive) and the memory track of a mind of a person who is dead (that is if the subject is dead).

(4) The directive once it has made connection, ceases to be of importance, its purpose has been fulfilled.

(5) The sensitive need not necessarily touch the directive though it can be helpful to do so. But as noted in Case V, a sheet of glass, or some smooth object, appears

to be an effective insulator if placed between the sensitive and the directive. (Miss Cummins finds touch necessary.)

(6) The more intense the emotional crisis the subject may have passed through, the more vivid the catastrophe, the stronger and more marked the personality, the more easily is the directive read. A murderer's knife, a thief's glove, a madman's watch, for example, are likely to yield interesting and positive results. In one case, a blindfolded sensitive was brought in contact with a large wooden bowl. She screamed and begged that it should be removed. It had been the sacrificial cup which King Thebaw had used to receive the blood of his many victims.

(7) The directive may be any small object, preferably one that has long been used or worn by the subject, or a specimen of his handwriting. The directive need not have been in the subject's possession immediately before, or even for a considerable time before the experiment is made but it will act, if the investigation is successful, as a directive to him as he is in the present time. In a reported case the investigation of the directive *led to* the discovery of his missing dead body.

(8) It will, of course, as stated previously, act as a directive to a dead owner, or the memory track he has left, equally with a living owner, so that both can be cognised. There may have been two or several owners of the directive being examined. Each owner can be cognised. Their records remain distinct. But here it depends to some degree on the relative "telepathic sensitivity" of the particular sensitive.

(7) One sensitive might prove more expert in one particular case than another. One might go deeper into the past and cognise an earlier owner of the directive. But each " subject " is always distinct and separate.

(An analogous condition is found with certain masseuses; one will be good for one case and fail with another).

The Sensitive

Somewhat as a bloodhound when shown a directive is able to follow a trail imperceptible to human senses so a sensitive when shown a directive can follow an equally *impalpable psychic trail* to Australia perhaps (Cases XIX or XX). Neither distance nor time appear to be barriers. Or again the trail may lead to ancient Spain (Case I and IX) or elsewhere. The sensitive's mind appears to work in some manner untrammelled by space or time, in fact "outside" of both. In regard to time, the sensitive can on occasion precognise events in the future of the one particular individual she is dealing with. All these ESP faculties depend in some degree on the capacity, development etc. of the particular sensitive employed, and the case and its nature that she is asked to investigate.

It would appear obviously easier to cognise and to retrocognise rather than precognise.

It is suggested that the sensitive sees the event associated with the subject's life as a picture, and translates the picture into words in her conscious mind. Much of her capacity to do this depends on the relative culture of her mind and the extent of the collection of word-pictures she may have stored in it.

The Subject

It would appear that each one of us, leaves an impress of our personality on every object with which we make contact in our life's journey. The impress may be slight, dim, transitory, but sometimes in emotional crises, the impress we leave may be very well marked, and the intensity of the crisis may leave a scar on the Race Memory that can be picked up later by a sensitive through the directive.

What is the nature of this scar, this trace that we appear to leave, this something that the sensitive can readily apprehend?—The sensitives' speak of "vibrations." "I am now getting in contact with this man's vibrations." Sometimes they speak of 'fluid,' of elements in which there may be 'light' and 'heat,' 'electric' or 'magnetic' currents or even smells, each differing from subject to subject.

These are simply terms that the sensitive uses to try and indicate in word-pictures what are the nature of extra sensory perceptions and apprehensions.

This intangible something that we leave as an impress on our belongings, has been said to be an impress on "the psychic aether" that is postulated as connecting mind and matter. But we must call a halt at this point. We leave on a directive something, that is of such a nature that it can be perceived, apprehended, traced, and differentiated by a sensitive. We have not progressed beyond this point at present, in our understanding of the process.

The hypothesis that has been advanced to cover the facts stated briefly is that the sensitive's mind can act at *different levels of significance,* that the sensitive stills her *conscious mind level of significance,* renders it quite passive, inactive. Then she allows her mind to act at *a different level of significance,* one that may be regarded as sub—or super— conscious. At this level she is said to be able to cognise the mind of the subject through the universal mind, which is postulated as lying behind or above or below or deeper than all phenomena, and it connects up all minds.

Finally the sensitive is able to translate the pictures she has seen of the subject, at the deeper *level of*

AN ADVANCE ASPECT OF ESP

significance of her mind, that she has been using, into words written or spoken through the *conscious level of significance of her mind,* that had remained passive. She interprets her vision in this manner to others. Does she tap a universal memory through a universal mind, or a universal mind from a universal memory? At least she brings back correct information not obtainable by other means.

Again to give a different analogy. An object has been contaminated by an atomic explosion, certain rays A,B,Y, etc. have passed through it. No apparent impressions remain. It is the same to a casual observer, as other objects, and yet it is highly dangerous. If a geiger-counter is passed over it, it at once reveals the condition of irradiation. It has become sensitized.

A sensitive can be likened to a geiger-counter. She is able to state that a directive has been 'irradiated' and she is able to describe (cognise) the personality that irradiated the directive—thus she gathers information about his personality and circumstances, etc.

The universal mind suggested to be at a deeper level of significance of the mind of the sensitive corresponds to *"The collective mind"* postulated by Jung. "The collective mind or common unconscious" according to Professor H. H. Price " is only another way of saying that at the deeper level of significance all personalities are in complete and continuous rapport."

But whatever the view taken of the universal mind, the collective mind, or common unconscious, the process of making contact with it is of major interest.

It may be asked again, is the information the sensitive discovers genuine? One example from Case I indicates this. From examining a document two-hundred years old for the first time, with two hardly decipherable names written on it in faded ink and over-written in an endeavour to preserve the lettering, her mind was capable of probing back through the centuries and obtaining accurate information concerning a man named Arias Davila, Bishop of Segovia, who had lived in the fourteenth century. The name had no significance to her or to the physician who employed her. No information concerning him could be obtained in local libraries, nor could his existence even be confirmed. Six months later confirmation was obtained by a research worker from a little-known reference book, Gratz's *Jewish Encyclopedia,* of which a translation is preserved in the British Museum. Three or four years later a full account of the more important events in this prelate's life were discovered by the author during an accidental perusal of Sabatini's work, *Torquemada and the Spanish Inquisition.* Still later the name Davila was observed in the press as belonging to a general prominent in the Spanish revolution.

All this information, including the name Davila, was given by the sensitive before confirmation of its truth or even of its existence was obtained. The facts recovered by her were proved to be true in every detail and they amply confirmed the remainder of the story of Juan Davila and his family. It was impossible to continue this research to its ultimate logical conclusion by the confirmation in addition of the latter's history, owing to the difficulty and expense of obtaining a reader capable of searching and deciphering the ancient Spanish records in the British Museum.

However, the discovery of unknown historic facts was amply proved. The name Davila, since proved to be connected with Spain, was recorded as such.

AN ADVANCE ASPECT OF ESP

In the face of such evidence it is impossible not to admit that a faculty of the mind exists capable of disclosing information not obtainable by the ordinary senses. Much other evidence of a similar nature could be given.

CHAPTER IV.

THE UNCONSCIOUS. AN ANALYSIS OF SOME CASES IN CHAPTER II. THE TRAINING OF SENSITIVES

However far into the boundless realms of the unconscious we may succeed in carrying the victorious invasion of the intellect, I fancy that we shall always reach a point at last at which the only practical policy consists of taking the unconscious on its own terms . . . allowing the unconscious to speak for itself.—*Toynbee.*

REFLECTING on this opinion, it is clear that the subject of the unconscious is so vast in its range, and the means of investigating it are so limited in their scope, that it is suggested that the unconscious must, on occasion, be allowed to speak for itself. Can this be done? It is suggested that by employing ESP, a further door is opened, for this purpose. Investigations of the ABC of the unconscious by ESP have been considered in Chapter I. A number of emotional stresses of a medical psychological nature have been considered in Chapter II. The method employed by an expert sensitive in investigating these cases has been described in Chapter III. It is claimed that both the methods and the results of this research indicate the truth of the above statement. By utilizing this method "The unconscious may be said to be made to speak for itself."

The sensitive and the investigator can be regarded as standing on the shore of the vast ocean of the unconscious. The sensitive, greatly daring, has ventured out into the flood and under the guidance of the directive has cast her line. She brings back to the shore her capture and submits it to the investigator. She does not herself know its nature, nor is it her business to interpret it. She hands it over to the trained physician to employ as he sees fit.

If some of the cases recorded in the above series are examined and analysed superficially, the first point that claims attention is that in all the more obscure of the cases, a succession of curiously apposite stories have been produced from the unconscious, differing widely from case to case, and from subject to subject, dipping back very often into the race history of the individual and uniting the past with the present, almost like piecing together the parts of a jig-saw puzzle. For example, why should a small boy scream and weep unexpectedly at the second inoculation of a diptheria vaccine, after a month's interval, at a year old, and some years later, when seeing the same doctor, while suffering from measles? It was ascribed to mere nervousness, and left at that, at the time.

So much so that some years later when investigating "nail biting" and unexplained nervousness in the same boy while the possible causes were mentioned to the sensitive (e.g. an air raid), the incident of the inoculation was quite forgotten, and yet she at once perceived it and wrote: " . . . It seems that this little boy had a needle stuck in him by a doctor when he was young" and she proceeded to point out how it connected up with a race memory of pain in a similar pattern, when his ancestors were stabbed by weapons used by their persecutors, in Ghettos, showing how amongst other causes, it augmented the nervous anxiety and the nail biting, expressing itself as Masochism.

Again why should an elderly retired bank manager rush to the window gasping for breath in the middle of the night, and object to anything tight around his

177

abdomen, and be nauseated by the smell of creosote, etc.? It would require an expert in writing detective romance to find explanations for all his symptoms. It would have been quite beyond the sensitive's conscious mind — and yet out of the unconscious, she records uniquely apposite explanations for each and every sympton and joins them in a consequential narrative. They are accepted at once by the bank manager, and he relinquishes his psychosis equally rapidly and much to the amazement of his medical attendant, and contrary to the sensitive's statement that as the case was of long standing it might be difficult to resolve in consequence.

Again of the two ladies who suffered from severe nervous asthma. In the first the sensitive traced the psychological cause of the asthma to an experience of agonizing breathlessness and fear that she suffered from, when as a little girl, she was chased by a young bullock in a high wind, up a steep hill in the dusk. No doubt a psychoanalyst would have discovered it, but none was available. In the second case, the sensitive associated as the primary cause of the Asthma a tragedy in a past age in Spain, associated with a confinement in suffocating circumstances, reinforced in a later age in a later ancestor, in Scotland, by imprisonment in similar conditions, and finally expressing itself as nervous asthma in descendants, (in a mother and two daughters in the latest generation.) A psychoanalyst would have uncovered this in time, but how long? In each case, each story was accepted as true and led to the disappearance of the asthma, when judiciously applied by the physician.

Again consider the stories that lay behind the Case of the Doodlebugs, the Man who upset the motor car, the case of the Dead Hands!—Consider the intricate and complicated collection of circumstances that built up their tragedies.

Consider the still more complicated tragedy of the writing inhibition; and again, the curious and complex race histories that filled the psychological backgrounds of the two patients in Australia and the disappointed doctor. Even with the most vivid of imaginations the sensitive could not have created in her conscious mind, solutions that would explain the complicated enigmas these cases presented so aptly. *It was necessary for her to look into their unconscious past and allow it to speak for itself.* Could all these details have been discovered by psychoanalysis, and in such detail and with such apposite explanation, that they were accepted as true, by all except the disappointed doctor, who had no wish to accept? We think not.

It is of interest in analysing these cases to observe how often the histories stretch back into the far past. The importance of the initial emotional stress, in casting the pattern of the future complex, is very evident. In the case of the dead hands this is illustrated clearly. It was impossible to overcome the emotional fear complex of the injured hand, by telling the patient of its trivial character, by X-raying it and displaying the normal bones, by giving him treatment and reassurance. It was necessary to trace right back to the severing of the hands of ancestors in a pogrom, and the firing of a Ghetto, before he was able to resolve his fears, by realizing the sinister association of the past with his own life experiences in the same pattern, and his accident. Yet he was quite unperturbed earlier by a severe injury to his eye threatening his sight! When the story was read to him he appeared to accept it as absolutely, as if he knew more about it than his physician who told him, which, no doubt, was in reality the case in his own subconscious.

Another aspect that should be noted in some of these cases is the intimate association between the mother and the unborn child. The mother's fears and anguishes seem to be shared or even transmitted to the unborn child.

In the first Case the pregnant mother was compelled to witness her husband's death by torture on the rack in horrible circumstances reflecting guilt on herself. The child was born while she was stated to have been insane from this experience.

In the case of periodic fasting the unborn child was impressed with the fear of life by a mother in the early stages of phthisis.

In the first Australian Case, a mother discovered that she was carrying the child of her husband's brother, who had been responsible for his murder, and knew it.

In an instance of Claustrophobia a fear of confined spaces was imposed on an unborn child, when her mother was rendered unconscious by smoke in a small room for a time.

Under deep hypnosis intra-uterine experiences are stated to have been recorded, but deep hypnosis is not looked on favourably as a means of investigation.

It is obvious that if these syndromes of intra-uterine experience are accepted then a more sheltered period of gestation should be insisted on. The psychological advice given at ante-natal clinics acquires greater significance.

All of these points emphasize the vital importance of probing the race history in cases of obscure psychoses.

It is useless to argue that a trained psycho-analyst could have dealt with all these cases, rapidly and without difficulty.   Experts are not found readily, still less twenty years ago, when this research was initiated. Patients have neither the time nor the means to submit to long and tedious analysis lasting for a year or more.   This is no effort to take away from or belittle the work of the psychoanalyst, far from it, but ESP should be of the greatest use to him. By short circuiting his investigations it would enable him to concentrate on his essential work, that of resynthetizing the personality of his patient, and of preventing any return of the emotional complex after its disclosure and resolution.   The strengthening, fortifying and building up the personality of his patient are essential after the crisis he has passed through.

The method of recovering Race Memories by free association, and by deductions from symbolic dreams must be, by its very nature a somewhat tedious and prolonged research.   ESP appears to be the only other method of obtaining the race history and in a single interview or its equivalent.   Even deep hypnosis does not probe beyond the individual life.

The physician is the first to come in contact with these obscure psychoses.   Many of the simple ones are dealt with by him in his daily work, if he can give them the time necessary. The medium ones can be dealt with by the psycho-analyst, but some of the cases recorded need more detailed investigation, and the psycho-analyst could be assisted by ESP, exercised by the sensitive, in a dramatic manner, in the writer's opinion.

In the cases recorded a general practitioner, in default of a specialist, had to deal with all of them.   He found the help of ESP essential.

If the method of its use could be developed it would be a boon to psycho-analyst and patient alike.

The patient would be saved prolonged examination extending over long periods of time, which could be harmful by over emphasizing the neurosis in the search for its cause and by creating "analysis addiction," as in the case of the disappointed doctor.

The series of cases described, though limited in number, suggest that fear and insecurity are the commonest of all causes of the emergence of paralysing emotional complexes, and this is what could be expected.

The need for food is the first and primary requirement of the living organism. The need for it takes priority. It precedes the need for sexual expression. Fear of the loss of food supply turns even the infant to its source, the mother. The loss would mean insecurity and ultimate starvation and extinction of the ego. Therefore any threat to the food supply creates emotional stresses from the very first. Fear of any competition for this basic source of nourishment from the father, or the family, would be a threat to continued existence, and would be resented vigorously. This natural fear appears to give a more rational explanation than the Oediphus and Electra fantasies, as primary causes of emotional complexes.

Again why should a blind kitten spit when a dog is brought near it? Is it Race Memories of insecurity and fear, or does it utilize its sense of smell? It is certainly a reaction to the primary fear of the extinction of the ego, which appears to be at the root of most psychoses.

The writer of these investigations into the application of applied ESP in medical psychoses was singularly fortunate in obtaining the services of an unusually expert sensitive.

How could a service of sensitives be established more generally, for those who are capable of utilizing them?

There are several very obvious difficulties in the way. Sensitives like the rest of the human race must live. They must therefore be given adequate remuneration for the specialized work they do. At present this is not the case. It takes time and patience to be trained. The work itself is time consuming and exacting. Some degree of culture and education is of importance. Two or three cases in a week is sufficient, because over-use of the ESP faculty produces exhaustion and lessens capacity. In consequence of these difficulties a service could only be established by setting up a central authority controlling a number of sensitives grouped under it. The central authority would call up each sensitive by rote when a service was required and would be in a position to guarantee the efficiency of the sensitive to the applicant and would determine that the applicant whether doctor or some other professional man, or woman, was thoroughly conversant with the method he was using and that he was actuated by a genuine and not a maleficient or frivolous purpose, and was prepared to pay an arranged fee for the service rendered.

The Department of Psychology in a University containing one, would be the proper authority to set up such a group of sensitives. It is their duty and purpose to investigate the range of the human mind. ESP in all its aspects appertains to the mind and is essentially their work.

The matter could be commenced by enrolling a number of sensitives recommended by some of the principal psychological societies. It should become a part of the authorities educational duties to train selected students in ESP. Commencing with the familiar card guessing experiments they should be guided fairly rapidly to the investigation of more difficult problems, because continuous repetition of tedious experiments tend to lessen rather than develop the faculty. Expert sensitives would guide and help promising students and the students could be added to the group as soon as they became efficient. It is not every candidate that would prove efficient, no more than every student of music will become a master. Nevertheless, with time and a demand, and financial security, it should be possible to build up a useful team of sensitives, and at the same time further the department of psychologists' own researches into the faculties of the human mind by the researches they would be carrying out with the sensitives.

The writer feels that such a group of sensitives properly controlled and supported would in time prove of incalculable value in research into various aspects of abstract knowledge.

These notes have been limited strictly to the medical aspect of the use of ESP. It is hoped that it will be taken up and utilized to a greater extent in the future for this and other purposes.

CHAPTER V

THE USE OF THE ESP FACULTY IN PSYCHOSES
Written from the unconscious by the sensitive.

The Process of ESP in Connection with Neurosis

THE directive or directives submitted to a sensitive are of the first importance, and as has already been shown care should be taken that they are not affected by alien memories.

When seeking general information about a certain person some sensitives appear to prefer a directive that has been intimately associated with an individual and reject his hand-writing.

In connection with persons suffering from neurosis, I have found that a specimen of the hand - writing of the patient is very often more helpful than any other directive that has been associated with him. It is of especial value if he writes something about his particular illness. It does not, however, appear to be the facts he writes about himself that are of service to the sensitive. In my experience if he even fairly briefly alludes to his sickness of mind in writing, his concentration on it gives a stronger impulse, a more immediate direction than anything else in relation to the particular field of memory that is sought. It is as a lead along the most direct road to the required destination. Or it might be likened to a magnet's power of attraction. In this instance, we may suppose that those facts that are the fundamental cause of the neurosis are attracted because ideas that are related tend to function as a unit.

A family heirloom, as for example the parchment granting the freedom of the City of London, can be of considerable service in the tracing of the racial inheritance. In the first rather obscure case mentioned the parchment had been intimately associated with numbers of the patient's ancestors in the direct line.

But it is too early yet to assert that any positive rule operates in respect of hand-writing as a favoured directive in psychometric analysis. Sensitives are not machines, they are individual in the measure and nature of their powers. It seems that the doctor can only find out by means of trial and error in co-operation with the sensitive employed, the most effective directive or lead to the required information about the patient.

A First Cause

In the practice of the ESP faculty our primary objective was to find the basic experience of fear which might be called the nucleus of the complex. The expression of the complex and its ramifications were not sought. It would require much inessential work, and, as has been shown in these cases, detail was not usually necessary to the cure.

Step by step the psychiatrist often tracks down through these ramifications, the fundamental cause of the neurosis.

In the method of ESP a short cut is taken, and many of what may seem to be necessary facts for the sound construction of the case are ignored. For this theory of treatment is based on the idea that in the majority of cases the instinct of self-preservation is stronger than any other. So the memories connected with it are the primary objective in the examination. Fear of the suppression of the ego may take many forms, but springs from the instinct of self-preservation. The orientation of the self, the establishing of it in its proper position in the world, is the one aim in view. Find, therefore, the envenomed spot, the primary fear, eliminate detail, which, though it may be useful, is not essential in the explanation given to the patient when resolution of the psychosis is sought. Indeed, detail may only arouse a certain morbidity which can be directly harmful in the mind of the patient, or it may merely confuse and tend to cloud the issues.

In these cases the sexual background of a neurosis has either been lightly dwelt on or, whenever possible, ignored. For there is a certain danger to the patient in an undue emphasis on sex. Sex has so many taboos it is not always safe or expedient to rouse this sleeping beast. The old Bible story of the house swept and garnished, into which entered far more wicked devils than the unclean spirit that previously occupied it, is an illustration of what may occur. Through over-emphasis of the sexual part of the trouble in the explanation and advice given to the patient a more harmful complex may be created. Indeed, whenever possible the void left by a complex should be circumvented by putting something wholesome in its place. It is vitally important to establish confidence or esteem for himself in the patient, and as far as possible to eliminate any sense of discouraging shame which might be roused by the detail of sex suppressions.

There is an illustration of how this difficult point was dealt with in the case* of a young girl who was suffering from a definite neurosis. The cause of it apparently lay in the fact that a man had once got into and slept in this girl's bed. The girl was religiously minded. In her unconscious mind this incident was symbolically illustrated. It was described as an event that had happened to the girl when she was a small child. "A bullying male had damaged an image of the Virgin Mary and had threatened the child with dire penalties if she ever told anyone of it." In this instance it seemed advisable to describe thus the symbol of the attack on virginity, rather than to tell the literal fact. The patient was a simple ignorant girl. There are cases, of course, in which it is possible to be quite frank. But such frankness requires a different emotional temperament and much greater intelligence than is found in many patients.

A First Cause

It may be pointed out that psychiatrists have cured numerous cases of neurosis by resolving sexual conflicts in the patients' subconscious minds. The reply to this is that the treatment of the symptoms was sufficient to bring back mental health through removing the cause of a feeling of insecurity. Basically associated in most cases with these conflicts is the insecurity fear. Features of sexual conflicts such as jealousy, hatred etc. so often spring from this fear, which is anxiety for the prestige of

* The incident was known to the physician in charge of the case, but not known consciously by the sensitive before she wrote the record. She used a small medal worn by the patient as her directive. She had been asked to write of the psychological background of the patient, as in all the cases already referred to, but not informed of the nature of the inhibitions that were suspected of being operative. In the record for the physician in charge, the sensitive gave only the above symbolic illustration of the incident, no reference to the true cause that it symbolized. This true cause was not mentioned by the sensitive until some weeks later, when this record with references to the use of the ESP faculty was obtained and it was referred to incidentally, as will be seen, merely to illustrate the possible danger of emphasising the sexual aspect of their difficulties to certain sensitive patients. This case has since recovered.

the ego, or fear of the results of loss of an individual's contribution to the well-being of the patient's ego, to its preservation in its wholeness.

Behind even the power and herd urges lurks the self-preservation or security instinct. Control of others, or domination of people gives a feeling of security and safety through the glorification of the ego.

Though it may not be necessary in a number of cases of neurasthenia to treat directly the fundamental self-preservation instinct it should be taken into account when treatment of any one of the other supposed causes of a neurosis fails. In other words, it is not necessary in numbers of cases to penetrate to the roots of being, to the fundamental desire to remain alive in satisfying security; the treatment of symptoms resolves the issue sufficiently to produce the patient's recovery.

The Void of Freedom

A very large number of people are afraid of freedom's loneliness. They therefore need some crutch to support them, they cannot stand by themselves. Free them from the fantasy that has caused the neurosis and they will in time, if you do not provide them with another healthier and more suitable fantasy, fall again and initiate a fresh neurosis.

Once the cause of the neurosis has been explained it is in the provision of a wholesome fantasy—whether it be in the mental processes connected with creative work or work for others—that in many cases a doctor best serves his patient. And accompanying such treatment there should be the strongly expressed auto-suggestion of belief in the patient's inherent powers. This is encouraging to the instinct of self-preservation, which needs more than the assurance of material safety and security for its satisfaction. It craves importance, it wants to matter considerably to others, for that too assures stability. The directive value of the doctor's efforts towards providing the patient with occupation and initiative in the acts of life is often half the battle in a permanent cure in that it caters for the need of the great instinct of self-preservation.

Man cannot live by bread alone. A deep sense of responsibility towards others, if acquired and properly directed, will make the self feel secure and worthy of self-preservation; the response of those others moved by the patient's fine creative work or his altruism will help to destroy the fundamental fear of negation, fear of the loneliness of death, because instinctively we feel that we are dead though we live, if we count for nothing either to the community or to any single human being.

There are of course, cases of strain in which the patient has been pressed too hard by his conscience, his sense of responsibility. He has to be made to relax, but that in itself must be created into an occupation for him. He should never be left to dwell in a void which the order for complete rest implies.

THE END

NOTE.—I have a wholetime occupation, so I only accept and work on cases of neurosis sent me by Dr. R. C. Connell, and he is in busy general medical practice and cannot undertake additional work of this character.

GERALDINE CUMMINS